First World War
and Army of Occupation
War Diary
France, Belgium and Germany

27 DIVISION
81 Infantry Brigade
Queen's Own Cameron Highlanders
2nd Battalion
18 December 1914 - 31 October 1915

WO95/2264/3

The Naval & Military Press Ltd
www.nmarchive.com
Published in association with The National Archives

Published by

The Naval & Military Press Ltd

Unit 10 Ridgewood Industrial Park,

Uckfield, East Sussex,

TN22 5QE England

Tel: +44 (0) 1825 749494

www.naval-military-press.com

www.nmarchive.com

This diary has been reprinted in facsimile from the original. Any imperfections are inevitably reproduced and the quality may fall short of modern type and cartographic standards.

© **Crown Copyright**
Images reproduced by permission of The National Archives, London, England, 2015.

Contents

Document type	Place/Title	Date From	Date To
Heading	WO95/2264/3		
Heading	27th Division 81st Infy Bde 2nd Bn Queen's Own Cameron Highlanders Dec 1914-Oct 1915		
Heading	81st Inf. Bde. 27th Div. Battn. Disembarked Havre From England 20.12.14 War Diary 2nd Battn. The Queen's Own Cameron Highlanders. December (18.12.14 To 31.12.14) 1914 Oct '15 Box 2264		
War Diary	Winchester	18/12/1914	19/12/1914
Miscellaneous	Roll of Officer statements for Action Service With 7 Battalion		
War Diary	Havre	20/12/1914	20/12/1914
War Diary	Aire	21/12/1914	31/12/1914
Heading	81st Inf. Bde. 27th Div. War Diary 2nd Battn. The Queen's Own Cameron Highlanders. January 1915		
War Diary	Aire	01/01/1915	05/01/1915
War Diary	Meteren	06/01/1915	06/01/1915
War Diary	Dickebusch	07/01/1915	09/01/1915
War Diary	Trenches	10/01/1915	10/01/1915
War Diary	Voormezeele	10/01/1915	10/01/1915
Miscellaneous	Scale to Saturday 9th January		
War Diary	Trenches	11/01/1915	11/01/1915
War Diary	Voormezeele	11/01/1915	11/01/1915
War Diary	Trenches	12/01/1915	12/01/1915
War Diary	Voormezeele	12/01/1915	12/01/1915
War Diary	Dickebusch To Westoutre	13/01/1915	13/01/1915
War Diary	Westoutre	14/01/1915	14/01/1915
War Diary	Westoutre to Groote Vierstraat	15/01/1915	15/01/1915
War Diary	Vierstraat	16/01/1915	19/01/1915
War Diary	Dickebusch	20/01/1915	20/01/1915
War Diary	Trenches	20/01/1915	21/01/1915
War Diary	Elzenwalle	21/01/1915	22/01/1915
War Diary	Dickebusch	22/01/1915	23/01/1915
War Diary	Westoutre	23/01/1915	28/01/1915
War Diary	Mille Kapelle (Dickebusch)	29/01/1915	30/01/1915
War Diary	Mille Kapelle (Dickebusch) To Trenches & Vierstraat	31/01/1915	31/01/1915
Heading	81st Inf. Bde. 27th Div. War Diary 2nd Battn. The Queen's Own Cameron Highlanders. February 1915		
War Diary	Trenches & Vierstraat	01/02/1915	01/02/1915
War Diary	Trenches & Vierstraat To Elzenwalle	02/02/1915	02/02/1915
War Diary	Elzenwalle	03/02/1915	03/02/1915
War Diary	Elzenwalle To Trenches & Vierstraat	04/02/1915	04/02/1915
War Diary	Trenches & Vierstraat	05/02/1915	05/02/1915
War Diary	Trenches & Vierstraat To Dickebusch	06/02/1915	06/02/1915
War Diary	Dickebusch	07/02/1915	07/02/1915
War Diary	Dickebusch To Trenches & Brasserie	08/02/1915	08/02/1915
War Diary	Trenches @ Brasserie	09/02/1915	09/02/1915
War Diary	Trenches @ Brasserie To Huts Mille Kapelle	10/02/1915	10/02/1915
War Diary	Mille-Kapelle To Reningheldst	11/02/1915	11/02/1915
War Diary	Reninghelst	12/02/1915	13/02/1915
War Diary	Reninghelst To Voormezeele	14/02/1915	14/02/1915

War Diary	Dickebusch	15/02/1915	15/02/1915
War Diary	Trenches (Bus-House) To Dickebusch	16/02/1915	16/02/1915
War Diary	Dickebusch	17/02/1915	17/02/1915
War Diary	Dickebusch To Trenches (Bus-House)	18/02/1915	18/02/1915
War Diary	Trenches (Bus-House)	19/02/1915	19/02/1915
War Diary	Trenches (Bus-House) To Dickebusch	20/02/1915	20/02/1915
War Diary	Dickebusch	21/02/1915	21/02/1915
War Diary	Dickebusch To Trenches (Bus-House)	22/02/1915	22/02/1915
War Diary	Trenches (Bus-House)	23/02/1915	23/02/1915
War Diary	Trenches (Bus-House) To Dickebusch	24/02/1915	24/02/1915
War Diary	Dickebusch	25/02/1915	25/02/1915
War Diary	Dickebusch To Trenches (Bus-House)	26/02/1915	26/02/1915
War Diary	Trenches (Bus-House) To Reninghelst	27/02/1915	27/02/1915
War Diary	Reninghelst	28/02/1915	28/02/1915
Heading	81st Inf. Bde. 27th Div. War Diary 2nd Battn. The Queen's Own Cameron Highlanders. March 1915		
War Diary	Reninghelst	01/03/1915	04/03/1915
War Diary	Reninghelst To Dickebusch	05/03/1915	05/03/1915
War Diary	Dickebusch	06/03/1915	06/03/1915
War Diary	Dickebusch To Trenches (Brasserie)	07/03/1915	07/03/1915
War Diary	Trenches (Brasserie)	08/03/1915	08/03/1915
War Diary	Trenches (Brasserie) To Dickebusch	09/03/1915	09/03/1915
War Diary	Dickebusch	10/03/1915	10/03/1915
War Diary	Dickebusch To Trenches (Brasserie)	11/03/1915	11/03/1915
War Diary	Trenches (Brasserie)	12/03/1915	12/03/1915
War Diary	Trenches (Brasserie) To Dickebusch	13/03/1915	13/03/1915
War Diary	Dickebusch To Brasserie (2nd Line)	14/03/1915	14/03/1915
War Diary	Brasserie (2nd Line) To Trenches (Brasserie)	15/03/1915	15/03/1915
War Diary	Trenches (Brasserie)	16/03/1915	18/03/1915
War Diary	Trenches (Brasserie) To Rosen-Hill Huts	19/03/1915	19/03/1915
War Diary	Rosen-Hill	20/03/1915	22/03/1915
War Diary	Rosen-Hill To Canada-Huts (Dickebusch)	23/03/1915	23/03/1915
War Diary	Canada-Huts	24/03/1915	31/03/1915
Heading	81st Inf. Bde. 27th Div. 2nd Battn. The Queen's Own Cameron Highlanders. April 1915		
War Diary	Canada-Huts (Dickebusch)	01/04/1915	01/04/1915
War Diary	Canada-Huts	02/04/1915	03/04/1915
War Diary	Canada-Huts To Trenches Ypres	04/04/1915	04/04/1915
War Diary	Trenches (Herenthage)	05/04/1915	07/04/1915
War Diary	Trenches (Herenthage) To Close Support Nr Sanctuary-Wood	08/04/1915	08/04/1915
War Diary	Sanctuary-Wood (Close Support)	09/04/1915	09/04/1915
War Diary	Sanctuary-Wood	10/04/1915	11/04/1915
War Diary	Sanctuary-Wood (Close Support) To Trenches (Inverness-Copse)	12/04/1915	12/04/1915
War Diary	Trenches (Inverness-Copse)	13/04/1915	15/04/1915
War Diary	Trenches (Inverness-Copse) To Ypres	16/04/1915	16/04/1915
War Diary	Barred @ Hooge	16/04/1915	16/04/1915
War Diary	Barred @ Ypres	17/04/1915	17/04/1915
War Diary	Ypres	17/04/1915	20/04/1915
War Diary	Ypres To Trenches S. E. of Zillebeke Tank	21/04/1915	21/04/1915
War Diary	Dugs-Outs Railway Cutting S. Of Zillebeke	22/04/1915	22/04/1915
War Diary	Died of W	05/05/1915	05/05/1915
War Diary	(Trenches Hill 6D)	23/04/1915	23/04/1915
War Diary	D. of W. 24th	23/04/1915	23/04/1915
War Diary	D. of W. 23rd	23/04/1915	23/04/1915

War Diary	D of W.25th	23/04/1915	23/04/1915
War Diary	D of W	03/05/1915	03/05/1915
War Diary	(Trenches) Zillebeke	24/04/1915	24/04/1915
War Diary	Zillebeke	25/04/1915	25/04/1915
War Diary	D of W 27/4	25/04/1915	25/04/1915
War Diary	Zillebeke	26/04/1915	26/04/1915
War Diary	Zillebeke (Trenches)	27/04/1915	28/04/1915
War Diary	Zillebeke Trenches To Support	29/04/1915	29/04/1915
War Diary	D of W	06/05/1915	06/05/1915
War Diary	D of W	04/05/1915	04/05/1915
War Diary	Potijze	30/04/1915	30/04/1915
War Diary	D of W.	01/05/1915	01/05/1915
Heading	81st Inf. Bde. 27th Div. War Diary 2nd Battn. The Queen's Own Cameron Highlanders. May 1915		
War Diary	Potijze	01/05/1915	01/05/1915
War Diary	D of W.	02/05/1915	02/05/1915
War Diary	Zouave Wood	02/05/1915	04/05/1915
War Diary	Hooge (Trenches)	05/05/1915	10/05/1915
Miscellaneous	Casualty List 10th May 1915	10/05/1915	10/05/1915
War Diary	Hooge (Trenches)	11/05/1915	11/05/1915
Miscellaneous	Casualty-List For 11th May 1915	11/05/1915	11/05/1915
War Diary	Hooge (Trenches)	12/05/1915	12/05/1915
War Diary	Hooge	13/05/1915	18/05/1915
War Diary	Heksken X Roads	19/05/1915	23/05/1915
War Diary	Heksken X Roads To Huts W Ypres	24/05/1915	24/05/1915
War Diary	Huts W. Ypres	25/05/1915	27/05/1915
War Diary	Huts W. of Ypres To Locre	28/05/1915	28/05/1915
War Diary	Locre To Steenwerk	29/05/1915	29/05/1915
War Diary	Steenwerk To Armentieres	30/05/1915	30/05/1915
War Diary	Armentieres	31/05/1915	31/05/1915
Heading	81st Inf. Bde. 27th Div. War Diary 2nd Battn. The Queen's Own Cameron Highlanders. June 1915		
War Diary	Armentieres	01/06/1915	02/06/1915
War Diary	Armentieres To Trenches Farm Du Biez	03/06/1915	03/06/1915
War Diary	Trenches Farm Du Biez	04/06/1915	07/06/1915
War Diary	Trenches (Fm Du Biez) To Armentieres	08/06/1915	08/06/1915
War Diary	Armentieres	09/06/1915	13/06/1915
War Diary	Armentieres To Trenches (Fm Du Biez)	14/06/1915	14/06/1915
War Diary	Trenches Fm Du Biez	15/06/1915	19/06/1915
War Diary	Trenches Fm Du Biez To Armentieres	20/06/1915	20/06/1915
War Diary	Armentieres	21/06/1915	26/06/1915
War Diary	Armentieres To Trenches (Fm Du Biez)	27/06/1915	27/06/1915
War Diary	Trenches (Fm Du Biez)	28/06/1915	29/06/1915
War Diary	Buried Chappelle D'Armentieres M16 Cemetery	29/06/1915	29/06/1915
War Diary	Trenches (Fm Du Biez)	30/06/1915	30/06/1915
Heading	81st Inf. Bde. 27th Div. War Diary 2nd Battn. The Queen's Own Cameron Highlanders. July 1915		
War Diary	Trenches (Fm Du Biez)	01/07/1915	02/07/1915
War Diary	Trenches (Fm Du Biez) To Armentieres	03/07/1915	03/07/1915
War Diary	Armentieres	04/07/1915	08/07/1915
War Diary	Armentieres To Trenches (Fm Du Biez)	09/07/1915	09/07/1915
War Diary	Trenches (Fm Du Biez)	10/07/1915	11/07/1915
War Diary	Trenches	12/07/1915	12/07/1915
War Diary	Trenches (Fm Du Biez)	13/07/1915	13/07/1915
War Diary	D of W. Erquinghem	13/07/1915	13/07/1915
War Diary	Trenches (Fm Du Biez)	14/07/1915	14/07/1915

War Diary	Trenches Fm Du Biez To Armentieres	15/07/1915	15/07/1915
War Diary	Armentieres	16/07/1915	16/07/1915
War Diary	Armentieres To Chapelle D'Amtn	17/07/1915	17/07/1915
War Diary	Ch. D'Armentieres	18/07/1915	18/07/1915
War Diary	Ch. D'Armentieres To Trenches (Fm Du Biez)	19/07/1915	21/07/1915
War Diary	Trenches Fm Du Biez	22/07/1915	26/07/1915
War Diary	Trenches (Fm Du Biez) To Ch. D'Armentieres	27/07/1915	27/07/1915
War Diary	Ch. D'Armentieres	28/07/1915	31/07/1915
Heading	81st Inf. Bde. 27th Div. War Diary 2nd Battn. The Queen's Own Cameron Highlanders. August 1915		
War Diary	Chapelle D'Armentieres	01/08/1915	01/08/1915
War Diary	Ch. D'Armentieres To Erquinghem-Lys	02/08/1915	02/08/1915
War Diary	Erquinghem	03/08/1915	15/08/1915
War Diary	Erquinghem To Trenches (Sq I 20. B.70)	16/08/1915	16/08/1915
War Diary	Trenches	17/08/1915	23/08/1915
War Diary	Huts (Rue Delettres)	24/08/1915	24/08/1915
War Diary	Huts	25/08/1915	29/08/1915
War Diary	Huts (Rue De Lettre) To Trenches (Bois Grenier)	30/08/1915	30/08/1915
War Diary	Trenches (Bois Grenier)	31/08/1915	31/08/1915
Heading	81st Inf. Bde. 27th Div. War Diary 2nd Battn. The Queen's Own Cameron Highlanders. September 1915		
War Diary	Trenches (Bois Grenier)	01/09/1915	02/09/1915
War Diary	Buried In Camebrin H.30.b.7.9.	02/09/1915	02/09/1915
War Diary	Trenches (Bois Grenier)	03/09/1915	05/09/1915
War Diary	Buried In Camebrin H.30.b.7.9.	05/09/1915	05/09/1915
War Diary	Trenches (Bois Grenier) To Huts-Rue Delettres	06/09/1915	06/09/1915
War Diary	Huts (Rue Delettres)	07/09/1915	08/09/1915
War Diary	Huts To Trenches (La Vesee)	09/09/1915	09/09/1915
War Diary	Trenches (La-Vesee)	10/09/1915	14/09/1915
War Diary	Trenches (La Vesee) To Huts (Erquinghem)	15/09/1915	15/09/1915
War Diary	Huts (Erquinghem)	16/09/1915	16/09/1915
War Diary	Huts (Erquinghem) To Bivouac (Vieux Berquin)	17/09/1915	17/09/1915
War Diary	Bivouac (Vieux Berquin)	18/09/1915	18/09/1915
War Diary	Vieux Berquin To Hazebrouck	19/09/1915	19/09/1915
War Diary	Warfusee-Abancourt	20/09/1915	20/09/1915
War Diary	Abancourt	21/09/1915	24/09/1915
War Diary	Abancourt To Proyart	25/09/1915	25/09/1915
War Diary	Proyart	26/09/1915	30/09/1915
Heading	81st Inf. Bde. 27th Div. War Diary 2nd Battn. The Queen's Own Cameron Highlanders. October 1915		
War Diary	Proyart	01/10/1915	07/10/1915
War Diary	Proyart To Trenches (Dompierre Sect)	08/10/1915	08/10/1915
War Diary	Trenches (Dompierre)	09/10/1915	11/10/1915
War Diary	Trenches (Dompierre) To Proyart	12/10/1915	12/10/1915
War Diary	Proyart	13/10/1915	15/10/1915
War Diary	Proyart To Cappy	16/10/1915	16/10/1915
War Diary	Cappy	17/10/1915	23/10/1915
War Diary	Cappy To Warfosee-Abancourt	24/10/1915	24/10/1915
War Diary	Abancourt	25/10/1915	25/10/1915
War Diary	Abancourt To Boves	26/10/1915	26/10/1915
War Diary	Boves To Bouganville	27/10/1915	27/10/1915
War Diary	Bouganville To St Aubin	28/10/1915	28/10/1915
War Diary	St Aubin	29/10/1915	31/10/1915
Map	Poelcappelle		
Miscellaneous	War Diary		

WO95/2264/3

27TH DIVISION
81ST INFY BDE

2ND BN QUEEN'S OWN
CAMERON HIGHLANDERS

DEC 1914 - OCT 1915

81st Inf.Bde.
27th Div.

Battn. disembarked
Havre from England
20.12.14.

WAR DIARY

2nd BATTN. THE QUEEN'S OWN CAMERON HIGHLANDERS.

D E C E M B E R

(18.12.14 to 31.12.14)

1 9 1 4

Box 2264

2nd Battalion The Queen's Own Cameron Highlanders.

Hour date and Place.	Summary of Events and Information.	Remarks & References to Appendices.
Winchester Dec 18 Friday 1914	Orders received to march to Southampton on 19th. Lts Patton Bethune & Gordon Cumming arrived from 3rd Bn Gordons – 3rd Bn. to take over details & stores left behind	

2nd Battalion The Queen's Own Cameron Highlanders.

Hour date and Place.	Summary of Events and Information.	Remarks & References to Appendices.
Winchester Dec. 14. Sat. 1914 9.60 am	Marched to Southampton route via Chandlers Ford. Arrived Southampton 2.30 pm. Road heavy - very wet. M.O. Grant & 30 men by train. Strength marching 28 Officers (doctor attached) 894 other ranks. 6 ASC attached 77 horses, 6 GS wagons, W[?] limbered wagon, 2 water carts, one Maltese cart. 13 men fell out all subsequently rejoined x 2 admitted to Hosp. Shirleton Embarked HT ATLANTIAN (Leyland Line) and Sailed at 6 pm. With Bde HQ & field Butchery on board. Rev. Gilchrist RC on board. Bn. Strength Embarking Officers 30 (2 attached) W.O. 1 Sgts 47 Dr 19 }919 Cpls 37 }871 Pts 875 M.Gs 4 GS Wagons 6 Lim " 15 W. Carts M. Carts	

Roll of Officers Embarked for Active
Service with 7 Battalion

Lt Col J Campbell DSO — Commanding
Maj AO Graeme — Second Major
"   PTC Baird
Capt W Maclean
"   RN Fraser
"   AD Macpherson — Adjutant
"   DM Crichton
"   R Campbell
"   RB Trotter
Lt   AL Macduff
"   HC Hepburn
"   AYG Thomson
"   AW Fowler
"   WE Nicholson
"   DG Davidson
"   JC Grant
"   LT Hussey-Macpherson
"   RAC Henderson
2 Lt JHR Anderson
"   HAH Dunsmure
"   A Fraser — Attached
"   D Grant   Capt B Biggar RAMC
"   J Murray   Rev ASG Gilchrist AC
"   JT Walker
"   J Gordon
"   A Fraser
"   G Hunter
Capt Jas D Macdonald — Quartermaster

2nd Battalion The Queen's Own Cameron Highlanders.

Hour date and Place.	Summary of Events and Information.	Remarks & References to Appendices.
Havre Dec. 20th Sunday 1914	Arrived off harbour 7 a.m. Disembarked 2 p.m. Good passage. Strength as for 19th. Bn. remained in wharf shed until 6.30 p.m - then marched to GARE MARITIME & entrained. Left Stn. 11 p.m. Capt Trotter, 4 Pltrs, 2 ASC, 4 Horses, 2 Wagons, left behind to follow. Fine - warm.	

2nd Battalion The Queen's Own Cameron Highlanders.

Hour date and Place.	Summary of Events and Information.	Remarks & References to Appendices.
AIRE. Dec. 21st Monday 1914	Arrived 8.30 pm. Met by Staff Capt. who conducted 3 Coys to Billets in French Penitentiary Bks. D. Coy followed later after unloading wagons. Last party arrived in billets at 2 pm. Accommodation on train 6 first class compartments for officers - men in trucks - 40 each truck. Horses in do - 8 in each. Wagons on open trucks 4 pr wheels to each.	

2nd Battalion The Queen's Own Cameron Highlanders.

Hour date and Place.	Summary of Events and Information.	Remarks & References to Appendices.
AIRE 22nd Dec. Tues 1914	Remained in Billets in "FORT" 4 p.m. Orders received to mount piquets guarding roads approaching from BOESEGHEM - N.W. Line taken up with 2 piquets - ½ Platoon A Coy each - from road junction ½ m. N of FORT to bank de Lys bank ¼ m. S.E. ¶ FORT frontage ¾ m. Piquets in position 5 p.m. withdrawn 8 a.m. Fine cold	

Adjutant

2nd Battalion The Queen's Own Cameron Highlanders.

Hour date and Place.	Summary of Events and Information.	Remarks & References to Appendices.
AIRE. 23rd Dec. Wed. 1914	Remained in Billets. Party sent out to dig positions for picquets. Picquets (1 Platoon coy) mounted 4.30 pm 5 pm orders received to reduce strength to 2 sections — owing to presence of 9th Bde Arty in neighbourhood of BOESEGHEM. Fine — some snow cold.	

2nd Battalion The Queen's Own Cameron Highlanders.

Hour date and Place.	Summary of Events and Information.	Remarks & References to Appendices.
AIRE 24th Dec. Thurs 1914	Remained in Billets Bn paraded at 9:30 am for Bde Route march distance about 11 m. returned to Billets 2.15 pm CO, Adjt & T. officers to Bde HQ 3 pm. Fine — warmer.	

I

2nd Battalion The Queen's Own Cameron Highlanders.

Hour date and Place.	Summary of Events and Information.	Remarks & References to Appendices.
AIRE 25th Dec Friday XMAS DAY 1914	Remained in Billets. 2nd WESSEX F. Coy. RE arrived 7 am & also took up quarters in Billets. Orders received to submit names of:— 2 Captains 2 Lieutenants 1 2/Lieutenant for transfer to 1st Bn. owing to shortage caused by recent casualties. following submitted. Capt D.Vm Crichton " R.T.S. Trotter Lt. H.C. Methuen " R.A.C. Henderson 2/Lt. A. Fraser H.M. the King's Xmas cards received & issued. Princess Mary's gifts of pipe & tobacco also being issued. Fine – Sharp frost.	B.M. 2.G. 25/7/14 returned

2nd Battalion The Queen's Own Cameron Highlanders.

Hour date and Place.	Summary of Events and Information.	Remarks & References to Appendices.
AIRE 26th Dec Sat. 1914	Remained in Billets. Coy Commrs. had close inspection of boots to ensure each man could wear them with 2 prs. socks. Fresh indents to replace submitted. Cold - damp, some rain fell after 4 pm. 2 Sick admitted to Hosp.	

2nd Battalion The Queen's Own Cameron Highlanders.

Hour date and Place.	Summary of Events and Information.	Remarks & References to Appendices.
AIRE. 27th Dec Sunday 1914	Remained in Billets Bn - two coys at a time - dug portion of entrenched position about 2½ m. N.E. AIRE. Cold - some rain in morning - fine later.	

Officers		30	31	1		30	
Other Ranks		919	976	57	1	6	
Horses { Riding		14	14				
Draught		55	56	1			Includes M.O. & Chaplain attached
Pack		8	8				C.O.R. 19h @ Base
M. Guns		4	4				
Wagons { 4-Wheeled		21	21				
2-Wheeled		3	3				
Bicycles		9	9				
	Effective Strength	War Establishment	Surplus to Establishment	Surplus attached	A.S.C.	Rations	

2nd Battalion The Queen's Own Cameron Highlanders.

Hour date and Place.	Summary of Events and Information.	Remarks & References to Appendices.
AIRE 28th Dec. Monday 1914	Remained in Billets. Bn. with remainder of Bde. continued line of trenches to South. Warmer. Some rain - Horses left.	A & B 1st Relief C & D 2nd

2nd Battalion The Queen's Own Cameron Highlanders.

Hour date and Place.	Summary of Events and Information.	Remarks & References to Appendices.
AIRE 29th Dec. Tues. 1914	Remained in Billets. Bn. with remainder of Bde. concluded line of trenches N. to CANAL D'AIRE. C & C Coy. fine. 1 man admitted Hospt. (total 3)	C&D 1st Relief A&B 2nd —

2nd Battalion The Queen's Own Cameron Highlanders.

Hour date and Place.	Summary of Events and Information.	Remarks & References to Appendices.
AIRE 30th Dec. Wed. 1914	Remained in Billets. Digging continued. Northern end of trench improved & "cover trench" dug. Following officers left @ 11.30am to join 1st Battn (vide Diary 25th Dec) Capt D.McCrichton " R.B. Trotter Lt. H.C. Methuen " R.M. Henderson 2Lt. Andrew Fraser Each officer accompanied by one servant. 74 men A.& S.H. attached, joined 1st Bn O. & S.H. Total decrease in strength 5 officers 79 men. Remaining with H.Qrs. Officers (including M.O. & Chapln) 25. Other ranks (excluding O.R. Sgt) 839 (less 3 in Aire Hosp[l]) Cold, Fine.	A&B 1st Relief C&D 2nd " Maj Baird Lt Macduff C.S.M. Cameron " McCallum proceeded to trenches for instruction

2nd Battalion The Queen's Own Cameron Highlanders.

Hour date and Place.	Summary of Events and Information.	Remarks & References to Appendices.
AIRE. 31st Dec. Thurs. 1914	Remained in Billets. Digging continued. Southern end of trenches improved & cover trenches dug. Barricades ordered on main roads & day picquet 1 NCO & 3 men mounted. Orders to stop all motor cars & examine passes. Cpt – D amp.	(7D 1st Reliefs Appx 2nd "

81st Inf.Bde.
27th Div.

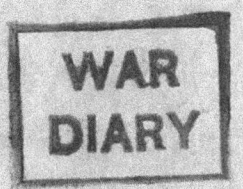

2nd BATTN. THE QUEEN'S OWN CAMERON HIGHLANDERS.

J A N U A R Y

1 9 1 5

2nd Battalion The Queen's Own Cameron Highlanders.

Hour date and Place.	Summary of Events and Information.	Remarks & References to Appendices.
AIRE. 1st January, 1915	Remained in Billets. Diary to date despatched to A.G's office Base. Digging continued at S end of trenches up to 1.15 pm. Bn. with remainder of Bde. formed up on both sides of Roman Rd. ½ m S. BOESEGHEM for inspection by Sir John French. C in C with Sir Horace Smith Dorrien & Divl Commander (Gen Snow) & Staff arrived 4 pm & inspected Bde. Bn returned to Billets 5 pm. 1 man admitted Hosp¹ (total 4) 15 unable to march Cold - Rain in afternoon. Maj Baird, Lt Macduff CSM Cameron & CSM McCallum returned from trip to trenches attached to DCLI	A & B 1/1/15

A.Phillips
Capt

2nd Battalion The Queen's Own Cameron Highlanders.

Hour date and Place.	Summary of Events and Information.	Remarks & References to Appendices.
AIRE 2nd January Sat 1915	Remained in Billets. Digging continued @ S. end of line. G.O.C. Bde. gave OC units line of 2nd Trenches on ground. Capt Maclean Lt Thomson C.S.M. Giffen " Christie proceeded to Trenches for instruction. Unable to march. Mild – Rain in morning.	C&D 1st Relief ATB 2nd "

2nd Battalion The Queen's Own Cameron Highlanders.

Hour date and Place.	Summary of Events and Information.	Remarks & References to Appendices.
AIRE. 3rd Jan: Sunday 1915	Remained in Billets. Digging continued in morning by ½ Bn, at N. end of line – A second position about 100x in rear of first being commenced. 2 men admitted to Hospt. (total 6) 10 unable to march 1 Draught horse died this morning. Mild – some rain	C&D 1 Relief.

STATE to SAT. Jan. 2nd

	Effective Strength	War Establishment	Wanted to Complete	Surplus	Civilian Billets	Sick	Rations
Officers	x25	x31	6				25
Other ranks	x830	967	137		1	6	
Horses Riding	15	15					
Horses H. Draught	12	12					
Horses Draught	41	42	1				
Horses Pack	9	9					
M. Guns	4	4					
Wagons 4 Wheel'd	21	21					
Wagons 2 Wheel'd	3	3					
Bicycles	9	9					

x Includes M. Officer & Chaplain
+ Includes Queen in Hospt. (6)

2nd Battalion The Queen's Own Cameron Highlanders.

Hour date and Place.	Summary of Events and Information.	Remarks & References to Appendices.
AIRE 4th Jan. Monday 1915	Remained in Billets. Orders received that 80th Bde. would move to Billeting area between HAZEBROUCK & BAILLEUL on 5th followed by 77th Bde on 6th & 82nd Bde on 7th. 27th Div'n eventually to occupy a line of trenches from St ELOI — GROOTE VIERSTRAAT about 3 miles S of YPRES. Each Bde in turn being in fire trenches - Reserve & Support in that order. 3 men to Hospt. (total 9) 5. Unable to march 2. M.G Horses sent sick. Weather - Wet.	

2nd Battalion The Queen's Own Cameron Highlanders.

Hour date and Place.	Summary of Events and Information.	Remarks & References to Appendices.
AIRE. 5th Jan: Tuesday 1915.	Remained in Billets. Orders received Bn would march 9 am leading Bde. Billeting party, 2nd in command, Interpreter, 4 C.S.Ms, 4 men (1 per Coy) 2 cyclists, to march at 7 am & meet Staff Capt at HAZEBROUCK. F.G.C.M. held on 2 Ptes & 5 Privates. To hospt 3 (total 12) left to march 6. Into — more rain	

2nd Battalion The Queen's Own Cameron Highlanders.

Hour date and Place.	Summary of Events and Information.	Remarks & References to Appendices.
METEREN 6th January Wed 1915	Marched from AIRE 9 a.m. Order of March Camerons, F.Coy RE, Argylls, R.Scots Gloucesters. — Route HAZEBROUCK, CAPPEL, CAESTRE, FLÊTRE. distance 18 miles. Road from MORBECQUE — pavé very rough in places. Very flat — arrived 4 pm About 300 new boots issued night previous to Marching — 1 absentee. (returned sick-ward) 3 admitted Hosp; (total 15) Strength marching out officers 25 others 821 Numbers (Excluded in above) unable to march 2 numbers fell out 31. Mild, some rain	

2nd Battalion The Queen's Own Cameron Highlanders.

Hour date and Place.	Summary of Events and Information.	Remarks & References to Appendices.
DICKEBUSCH 7th January Thurs 1915	Marched from METEREN 8.50 am to starting point 1/4 M.W. of BAILLEUL Order of March KSLI (81st Bde) Adv Gd, A&SH, Camerons, 2nd Worc & 71 R.E. 20th R.F.A Bde, T Amm Col.th, 2nd Glosters, 1 R. Scots. Route via BAILLEUL, LOCRE, WESTOUTRE, REMINGHELST, OUDERDOM. ~~Mountain~~ direct road from LOCRE not taken as too exposed to enemy's fire. Column halted S.E 1 m. from OUDERDOM @ 1.35 pm until 4.30 pm. Some enemy's arty fire observed in direction of line VOORMZEELE - VIERSTRAAT 6000x. Bn arrived in Billets 7 pm. Transport, Echelon B, 8.30 pm Train transport continued to arrive up to 11 M/N (one water cart 5/Bn) 8th Bn ordered to be prepared to support Bde at road junction 1 3/4 m. N.E Billets - at which place 1/A&SH. were bivouaced supporting KSLI in VOORMZEELE (S of Lake) Divn. Trench line (taken over by 80th Bde on 7th from French troops) from ST ELOI on N. to point 1 m SE VIERSTRAAT on S. 1 absentee	
	1 Numbers marching Officers 25 O.Rks	P 9
	2 Numbers available to march 3 (included in above)	
	3 Numbers marching separately (included in (1))	14
	4 Numbers Fell out	6
	Cold. Heavy Rain	

2nd Battalion The Queen's Own Cameron Highlanders.

Hour date and Place.	Summary of Events and Information.	Remarks & References to Appendices.
DICKEBUSCH 8th January 1915	Remained in Billets Bde in support of 80th Bde in trenches as described in Diary of yesterday & attached sketch. A & S.H. pushed out to X Roads 1 M. N.E. of village. In afternoon fatigue went out to collect material for trenches.	
State	off. Officers Hosp. to H. sick unfit Total 23 / 823 / 15 / / 29 - 8 / 37 /	

2nd Battalion The Queen's Own Cameron Highlanders.

Hour date and Place.	Summary of Events and Information.	Remarks & References to Appendices.
DICKEBUSCH 9th January 1915	Remained in Billets in Support - as on Friday - Collected more material for trenches. Order received to occupy trenches on following day.	
State	Off. Other Horses 25/823/15 ✓ Left oudaw / Sick to March 10 / inft to 3	2 draught horses required to complete
	Cold. Rain.	

2nd Battalion The Queen's Own Cameron Highlanders.

Hour date and Place.	Summary of Events and Information.	Remarks & References to Appendices.
TRENCHES Voormezeele 10th January Sunday 1915	Coys moved out to Trenches in following order - taking over from 4th K.R.R. B. Coy. 4:30 pm C. " 4:45 pm A. " 5:0 pm D. " 5:30 pm Transport followed C.Coy who took over supporting trenches. Transport remained at X roads KREUSSTRAATHOEK from which place supplies & material were carried to VOORMEZEELE at which place Bn. H.Q. were established in a cellar close to Regtl. Aid post. Relief of trenches completed without casualties by 12 mn. Coys taking over from K.C.L in order B. A. D. K.R.R. Bn H.Q. @ St ELOI abandoned as being unsuitable - K.R.R. having been 3 days in trenches showed great signs of distress - large numbers being unable to walk Cold but	

2nd Battalion The Queen's Own Cameron Highlanders.

Hour date and Place.	Summary of Events and Information.							Remarks & References to Appendices.
	State to Saturday 9th January							
	Officers	25ˣ	31ˣ	6			25	
	O.Ranks	823	976	153	1	6	830	
Horses {	Riding	15	15			15		
	H. Draught	12	12			12		
	Draught	72	42	3		39		
	Pack	9	9					
	M.G.	4	4					
Wagons {	4 wheeled	21	21					ˣ Jackson and Chaplain
	2 Wheeled	3	3					
	Bicycles	9	9					
	Effective Strength War Establ^t heads to Complete Surplus Civilian all out R.S.C. Returned							

AWright
CO 2/

2nd Battalion The Queen's Own Cameron Highlanders.

Hour date and Place.	Summary of Events and Information.	Remarks & References to Appendices.
TRENCHES 11th January 1915. VOORHEZEELE	Bn. occupied trenches taken over yesterday. Nothing of interest reported. Support Trenches received some shelling. Casualties wounded 4 died of exposure 2 X No. 9240 Pte LYALL A. " 7220 " REID A. ~~…~~ " 9169 " CARLYLE D. " 8312 " McLANEY A. ○ No. 8098 " STALLARD A. " 6396 " KING A. Mud in trench terrible, presents serious menace to general safety – witness 2 men who fell forward in it & could not move & were suffocated. Packs being carried added greatly to difficulties & hampered units movements. One Platoon D. Co. relieved by supports & returned to H.Q. By day no movement outside	

2nd Battalion The Queen's Own Cameron Highlanders.

Hour date and Place.	Summary of Events and Information.	Remarks & References to Appendices.
11th	Trenches could take place & little done within them — consequently all communication, parties for rations & material, working parties &c had to move at night. Sniping at night fairly continuous commencing at dusk gradually dying down towards dawn & generally ceasing altogether in the daytime. Shell fire on the contrary commenced @ dawn & continued intermittently by day — only a very occasional round being fired @ night. With the exception of support trenches most of Arty. fire was directed on batteries situated along a line from 1000 to 2000 yds in rear of fire trenches. One battery (French) immediately behind Bn. H.Q.	

2nd Battalion The Queen's Own Cameron Highlanders.

Hour date and Place.	Summary of Events and Information.	Remarks & References to Appendices.

11th — in VOORMEZEELE receiving particular attention.

A Store was established in VOORMEZEELE to which place all rations were carried from X Rds @ KREUSSTRAAT HOEK & divided up according to the numbers in the various trenches. They were then carried down to trenches.

A time table was made out for movements of Ration parties & S.B. parties to avoid having too many moving along trench roads @ one time.

Telephone C.M. was never established from trenches to Bn Hq & though that from Bn. to Bd. Hq was @ first complete it afterwards broke down. Consequently all C/ion had to be kept up by orderlies.

Sick & wounded evacuated through Amb. @ X Rds. K. HOEK.

Erlott Wel

H D McCall
Capt
Adjt

2nd Battalion The Queen's Own Cameron Highlanders.

29

Hour date and Place.	Summary of Events and Information.	Remarks & References to Appendices.
TRENCHES 12th January Tues 1915 VOORMEZEELE	Bn. occupied Trenches. As on previous day C. Coy in Support had some shelling. Trench occupied by Lt. Grant hit & earth fell in, no casualties however though officer & men were smothered in debris. Early in morning & again after dark sick & wounded were brought in from trenches. <u>Died of Wounds</u> (1) No 7545 Pte James Bain C Coy <u>Wounded</u> (5) 7927 Pte R. Curtis B 1677 L/Cpl W. Storey B 7555 Pte J. Russell B 8782 L/Cpl J. Fraser D 8092 Pte W. Keir B Shiping continuous during the darkness till day light when as before it ceased shell fire began. Bn. relieved by Leinster Regt. (82nd Bde) relief commencing at 7.30 pm & going on until 2 AM 13th	

2nd Battalion The Queen's Own Cameron Highlanders.

Hour date and Place.	Summary of Events and Information.	Remarks & References to Appendices.
12th	Condition of men coming out pitiable. Numbers could scarcely walk & all were perished with cold, & caked with the most stinking mud from head to foot, & soaked to the skin. Enemy evidently got information of relief for they became most active sniping heavily & opening shell fire on road leading from trenches to H.Q.	
	The Chaplain came out from DICKEBUSCH & read service over late Pte King who was buried in VOORMEZEELE church yard - just inside & close to railing on right of main entrance from road.	
	Pte Bain ~~Hallard~~ was buried just behind his trench by his section. Pte Hallard's body was not recovered.	
	The last party got into Billets in DICKEBUSCH @ 4 p.m. 13/1/15. all cold & wet.	

2nd Battalion The Queen's Own Cameron Highlanders.

Hour date and Place.	Summary of Events and Information.	Remarks & References to Appendices.
DICKEBOSCH to WESTOUTRE 13th January 1915	At 5.30 pm. Bn. was relieved from Support & Bns marched independently to Reserve Billets — Gloucesters @ Mt. KOKEREELE R. Scots between this & WESTOUTRE Cameron Bn. WESTOUTRE, A.T.S.H. REHINGHELST — ZEVECOTEN — HEKSKEN — Arrangements were made to carry men unable to march (104) in wagons. Bn. arrived WESTOUTRE at 9 pm, march much delayed as no arrangements were made by Bdes (80th & 81st) for times for moving to. Billets very scattered & officers billets very dirty & confined local inhabitants do not appear at all friendly or obliging. This is very noticeable since crossing the Belgian Frontier. Cold & wet	

25 / 737 / 80 - of whom 6 admitted since 10th & 1 man discharged

2nd Battalion The Queen's Own Cameron Highlanders.

Hour date and Place.	Summary of Events and Information.	Remarks & References to Appendices.
WESTOUTRE 14th January. Thurs 1915	Remained in Billets Nothing to Chronicle occurred. Cold - wet -	

H D Milan
ADjt

2nd Battalion The Queen's Own Cameron Highlanders.

Hour date and Place.	Summary of Events and Information.	Remarks & References to Appendices.
WESTOUTRE to GROOTE VIERSTRAAT 15th January Friday 1915	At 4.20 p.m. Bn. marched to Dickebusch there splitting up — two Coys (B & C) going on to VIERSTRAAT & LA BRASSERIE respectively — the left & centre of Divisional trench line. A & D Coys & M. guns remained in Dickebusch. The whole Bn. was in close support of 80th Bde. Bn. HQ established in "Dugout" at Vierstraat. Relieved 18th Royal Irish. Composite Bn. formed @ Brasserie (Bun HQ) of all men unable to march — Bn. contributed 83. With this party went Lt. Grant A/D Coy. Relief carried out & completed by 10.30 pm without casualties.

Cold day — rain later | |

2nd Battalion The Queen's Own Cameron Highlanders.

Hour date and Place.	Summary of Events and Information.	Remarks & References to Appendices.
VIERSTRAAT 16th January Sat 1915.	Bn. continued in close support to Trenches. During evening 80th Bde were relieved by 77th. Enemy quiet. No. 8305 Pte S/Laing Bty. reported as having accidentally shot himself in hand — wound serious.	

Officers	25		31	6			25	
Others	810	15	976	166		1	817	Not 15 Wounded 10
Horses { Riding	42½	15	42				15	
H. Draught		12	12				12	
Draught	9	42	9				42	1
Pack							9	9
M.G.	4	2	4				2	
Transport { 4 Wheeld	21	9	21				9	
2 Wheeld	3		3					
Bicycles	9		9					
	Effective Strength	War Establt.	To Complete	Surplus Attached	Attached			

2nd Battalion The Queen's Own Cameron Highlanders.

Hour date and Place.	Summary of Events and Information.	Remarks & References to Appendices.
VIERSTRAAT 17th January 1915	Bn. continued in close support to 81rd Bde. Some Artillery firing broke out after 2 am (presumably French) in N. direction & continued for about ½ hr. Subsequently heard that Gloucester H.Q had been heavily shelled until enemy's guns were silenced by ours & French. Throughout day artillery fire on both sides fairly continuous, directed mostly against each other. Fine morning - hail & snow later.	

2nd Battalion The Queen's Own Cameron Highlanders.

Hour date and Place.	Summary of Events and Information.	Remarks & References to Appendices.
VIERSTRAAT 18th January Monday 1915	Bn. remained in close support to 87th Bde. until evening when 82nd Bde relieved those in trenches. No alteration in dispositions of Coys at VIERSTRAAT & LA BRASSERIE. B. Coy at former place was occupied during darkness in improving & making defensible the existing French trench running along S.E. edge of road to LA BRASSERIE. At about 9 p.m. Enemy's Arty. which had been quiet during day opened on guns in rear of VIERSTRAAT & continued heavy fire over village for ½ hr. Fine day — some snow fell: cold.	

2nd Battalion The Queen's Own Cameron Highlanders.

Hour date and Place.	Summary of Events and Information.	Remarks & References to Appendices.
VIERSTRAAT 19th January Tuesday 1915	Remained in close support to 82nd Bde. At 11 am enemy shelled over village but did no material damage. C. Coy @ BRASSERIE also received some shelling. At 4.30 pm A coy relieved B @ VIERSTRAAT & D relieved C. at BRASSERIE. B & C returning to DICKEBUSCH with Bn H.Q. Wet & Cold	

2nd Battalion The Queen's Own Cameron Highlanders.

Hour date and Place.	Summary of Events and Information.	Remarks & References to Appendices.
DICKEBUSCH 20th Jan: Wed 1915 TRENCHES	Bn. remained in close support to 82nd Bde until evening when the 81st Bde relieved 82nd in trenches. As before Bn. occupied left section adjoining FRENCH (142nd Bde of 31st Div) B Coy on Right, A & 1 sect MGun in centre & D on left. C Coy in support & 1 section in H.Q. Casualties while relieving wounded. 1994 Pte J. Skinner C Coy 9344 " J. Moran B " Relief carried out fairly quickly with little snipping & no arty: fire Trenches found in very bad state indeed particularly on left — Communication by telephone to trenches not established No 7549 Pte C. Day C Coy Accidentally wounded in foot (self inflicted) Very Wet & cold	

2nd Battalion The Queen's Own Cameron Highlanders.

Hour date and Place.	Summary of Events and Information.	Remarks & References to Appendices.
TRENCHES 21st Jan. Thursday 1915 to ELZENWALLE	Bn. held trenches. HQ in VOORMEZEELE. At 2.40 am message came from O.C. D. Coy (left section) reporting enemy's sap had reached trench & asking for support. This was however cancelled in about half an hour as it proved to be a mistake. From 10.30 am to 1 pm Enemy's Artillery kept up continuous fire on ground 300 yds N.E. of VOORMEZEELE — presumably searching for French battery which was finding a position about there. Battn relieved by 1/A&SH at 6 pm. Relief completed about 12 mn. Bn. moving back to close support. HQ & M.G. A & D Coys @ ELZENWALLE, C. Coy - CHATEAU 400 x N.W. KREUSSTRAAT, B. Coy BRASSERIE on VIERSTRAAT Road. Casualties during day No. 9245 Pte. F Sinclair B Coy. Died - sitting in dug-out which collapsed & fell in on him. 2 Lt. T. WALKER wounded (h. gun) No. 7888 Sgt. Macdonald D Coy " 5202 " L Spencer A Coy As on former occasion much material sent up to trenches for repairs Cold — much rain	

2nd Battalion The Queen's Own Cameron Highlanders.

Hour date and Place.	Summary of Events and Information.	Remarks & References to Appendices.
ELZONWALLE 22nd January Friday 1915 to DICKEBUSCH	Bn. was in close support to 1/A.&S.H. dispositions as for 21st. At 2.30pm. 200 men were turned out to commence a second line of trenches behind BRASSERIE in woods. At 7.30pm. Bn. relieved by Royal Irish & returned to Billets in DICKEBUSCH. From previous evening a Report Centre was established at KREUSSTRAATHOEK to maintain communication between Trenches & Bde Hq in D-BUSCH. Fine - Cold	

2nd Battalion The Queen's Own Cameron Highlanders.

Hour date and Place.	Summary of Events and Information.	Remarks & References to Appendices.
DICKEBUSCH 23rd January Sat 1915 to WESTOUTRE	Bn. remained in billets until 5.20 pm when it moved to WESTOUTRE - 5½ m. Transport left before Bn. Bn. arrived WESTOUTRE 8pm "going" very bad & marching very slow owing to condition of men's feet after trenches. 1 Officer & 4 men carried on wagons. Bn. to remain for 6 days in Reserve to West. Fine Cold	

	Effective	Brooke	War Estab.	Complete	Happt. field	Base	Attached	Rations	
	9 3 21 4 9 12 41 15 598 23		30 1	9 3 2 9 8 12 42 15 976 31	1 - - - 1 - - - 358 1		14 1	192 1	
							9 12 41 15 625 23 7		x Indians + Pte Chaplain

2nd Battalion The Queen's Own Cameron Highlanders.

Hour date and Place.	Summary of Events and Information.	Remarks & References to Appendices.
WESTOUTRE 24th Jan. Sunday 1915	Bn. occupied Billets in Reserve. 1 NCO & 8 men returned fit from BOESCHEPE Fine - Cold	

2nd Battalion The Queen's Own Cameron Highlanders.

43

Hour date and Place.	Summary of Events and Information.	Remarks & References to Appendices.
WESTOUTRE 25th Jan Monday 1915	Bn. remained in Billets. — In parties of 50 under an Officer Men were marched to BOESCHEPE to wash. Each man after bathing was given a change of underclothing. BOESCHEPE distant 3 miles, 23 Men unable to march were collected & carried in wagons Lt Anderson sent to Hospl. (Pvt) Lt Macduff " " Composite Bn. Boeschepe Fine — Colo.	
WESTOUTRE 26th Jan: Tuesday 1915	Bn. remained in Billets — Fatigue parties employed on R.E. work as on 25th Orders received that owing to Kaiser's birthday Germans likely to deliver a strong attack on our line — Bde therefore to stand by for 48 hrs. to move in support at moments notice. After dusk till early morning heavy firing heard on left of our line or in French lines. Lt. Grant returned from Boeschepe. Fine — Colo.	

2nd Battalion The Queen's Own Cameron Highlanders.

44

Hour, Date and Place.	Summary of Events and Information.	Remarks & References to Appendices.
WESTOUTRE 27th January Wed 1915	Remained in Billets - Fatigues as on two previous days. State 		Officers	Others	In Hospl	To Hospl	Off Sick
Present	23	570	206	5	1/33
Boeschepe	1	20			
Base		1				 Cold Fine	Frost
WESTOUTRE 28th January Thurs 1915	Remained in Billets - 10 men tried by F.G.C.M. STATE 		Off	Men
Present	21/2	546
BOESCHEPE	1	40
Sick in H.	2	233
" with unit		14
BASE		1
Command.		1
	25	835 | 2/Lt Walker × Lt Anderson 4 draught Horses to complete Cold Fine Frost
MILLE KAPELLE (DICKEBUSCH) 29th Jan - Frid 1915	Bn. marched to MILLE KAPELLE with Bde - to relieve 72nd Bde in support of trenches. Bn. occupied New huts constructed by R.E. in wood. Huts made of logs & tarpaulins roof & floor, with hurdles along centre - size about 17'×12'×8' one end closed by iron sheet. Left Westoutre 5.30 p.m arrived billets 8 p.m. 5 men carried - 3 men fell out State 		Off	men
Present	20	550
BOESCHEPE	1	40
Sick in H.	4	236
" with unit		1
Base & Comt.		2
	25	835 | 2/Lt Walker 2/Lt Anderson, Capt Macdonell, Capt Campbell. 4 draught horse to complete Cold - Fine - Frost - later Snow.
MILLE KAPELLE (DICKEBUSCH) 30th Jan: Sat. 1915	Bn. remained in Billets. At 12.30 am heavy Rifle & Artillery fire broke out in direction N. of Hill 60. Bn. ordered to stand by ready to support if necessary but in an hours time firing died away. |	Off	Others	Horses	Wagons	B.D	Pack	M.G.	B.W. Carts	G.S. Carts	Bicycles
Effective Strength	20	554	15	38	12	9	4	21	3	9
BOESCHEPE	1	43								
WAR estab.	31	976	15	42	12	9	4	21	3	9
To complete	10	379	✓	4	✓	✓	✓	✓	✓	✓
Hosp Wounded	1	14								
Sick	3	222								
Base & Comd.		2								
Attached		7								
Rationed	20	561	15	38	12	9	✓	✓	✓	✓	 Inclum. M.O. & Chaplain Cold - Some Rain - Thaw.

2nd Battalion The Queen's Own Cameron Highlanders.

Hour, date and Place.	Summary of Events and Information.	Remarks & References to Appendices.
MILLE KAPELLE (DICKEBUSCH) to TRENCHES @ VIERSTRAAT 31st Jan. Sunday 1915	Remained in Huts until 5 pm when C Coy moved to Trenches in front of VIERSTRAAT followed @ 1/4 hr. interval between Coys by B, D & A — to Relieve 1/R. Scots. C Coy took over left section, B centre & D right. A Coy was in support @ VIERSTRAAT with H.Q. Found trenches slightly improved with the exception of C (left) Coy's to which little had been done. Relief carried out by 10 pm Enemy quiet Casualties during Relief Wounded. No. 8532 L/Sgt J. Duncan C Coy " 7510 Dr. J. MILNE C " Thaw & Cold – Bright moon.	

	Offr	O Ranks
Present	20	547
BOESCHEPE	1	46
Sick in Hosp	4	238
With unit	/	/
Base & Coast		4
	25	835

This was the first time Gumboots & Whale Oil were issued — whether as result of this or from other causes – result in fewer cases bad feet — most satisfactory.

81st Inf.Bde.
27th Div.

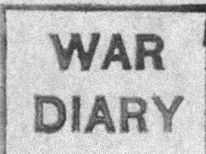

2nd BATTN. THE QUEEN'S OWN CAMERON HIGHLANDERS.

F E B R U A R Y

1 9 1 5

2nd Battalion The Queen's Own Cameron Highlanders.

N79th

Hour, Date, and Place	Summary of Events and Information	Remarks and References to Appendices
TRENCHES @ VIERSTRAAT 1st Feb. Monday 1915.	Bn. occupied trenches – nothing of special interest occurred – [D Coy on right received some shelling – one shell bursting on parapet of support dug-out without inflicting any damage to occupants.] During night 31/1 – 1/2 much work was done in improving & repairing trenches & in putting out barbed wire "knife-rest" entanglements. The Coy in Support @ VIERSTRAAT was divided into two reliefs – one to work by day in collecting & making material to be carried down by night by the other relief. The experiment of sending out during night, hot coffee in Rum jars proved most satisfactory. The coffee was made in DICKEBUSCH and re-heated in VIERSTRAAT whence it was carried to trenches – the jars being retained for filling with water for use during day. Draft of 1 officer (2nd Lt. MacFadyen 3/CH) and 141 other ranks joined from 3rd Battn. INVERGORDON.	

2nd Battalion The Queen's Own Cameron Highlanders.

7/79th

Hour, Date, and Place	Summary of Events and Information	Remarks and References to Appendices
TRENCHES @ VIERSTRAAT to ELZENWALLE 2nd Feb. Tues. 1915	Occupied Trenches during day until relieved by 1/R. Scots at 7 pm. Relief completed 11 pm [Coys moving independently to ELZENWALLE - D Coy & M. Gun to BRASSERIE. Relief carried out] without casualties. Draft came out from DICKEBUSCH & kept at BRASSERIE for fatigues during night. Fine - wet later.	

2nd Battalion The Queen's Own Cameron Highlanders.

2/79th

Hour, Date, and Place	Summary of Events and Information	Remarks and References to Appendices
ELZENWALLE 3rd Feb. Wed. 1915	Bn. remained in close support with D Coy & M. Gun at BRASSERIE - [At dawn men of draft of A.B.C. Coys joined their Coys. from BRASSERIE.] Day was spent in collecting material & making wire entanglement & stakes for trenches. [Also in cleaning up billets which were found - as usual in the most filthy condition. Enemy's Aeroplanes active during morning & afternoon - but cleared off about 4 pm. Work in consequence much hindered as when their presence is notified by look-out men with whistle every one has to knock off & conceal himself.] Fair day - Cold.	

2nd Battalion The Queen's Own Cameron Highlanders.

7/79th

Hour, Date, and Place	Summary of Events and Information	Remarks and References to Appendices
ELZENWALLE to TRENCHES @ VIERSTRAAT. 4th Feb. Thurs. 1915	Remained in close support till evening when we relieved 1/R. Scots in same trenches @ VIERSTRAAT. [During night 3/4th at 2.20 am a message was received from Bde HQ. that enemy had pierced line of 28th Divn N. of canal above St ELOI. Bn. stood to arms for 2 hours when orders came to turn in] Work during day continued as on 3rd about 3 pm. Capt. J.G. Ramsay arrived & took over A. Coy. During afternoon enemy commenced shelling village without doing any damage beyond breaking a few tiles. Relief ordered to commence @ 5.15 pm. was postponed at last minute & Bn. stood by to move in support of Left (St ELOI) Section which was reported threatened. Report proved groundless & orders to carry on received about 10.30 - Relief eventually completed at 12 m.n. No casualties. Fine cold. rain later.	

2nd Battalion The Queen's Own Cameron Highlanders.

2/79th

Hour, Date, and Place	Summary of Events and Information	Remarks and References to Appendices
TRENCHES @ VIERSTRAAT. 5th Feb. Friday 1915	Bn. occupied trenches as on former occasion (1st & 2nd ½ A Coy in support working continuously at material the other half carrying to trenches by night.) Trenches on left & right shelled - right ones heavily [C.H.E. with trenches established + valuable information of effect of our Arty fire on enemy's position passed to Arty. observing officers.] Casualties during day 2 Killed. (Rifle bullet) No 8301 Pte E. Gall D Coy " 7091 Pte A. Sinclair B. " Both these men were buried in field S.E. of cross roads ¼ m. N.W. of VIERSTRAAT graves dug about 50 and 75 yds in from WYTCHAETE & NEUVE-EGLISE Roads respectively Rev. A. Gilchrist conducted service Fine - Cold.	

2nd Battalion The Queen's Own Cameron Highlanders.

7/19th

Hour, Date, and Place	Summary of Events and Information	Remarks and References to Appendices
TRENCHES @ VIERSTRAAT to DICKEBUSCH 6th Feb. Sat. 1915	Beyond some shelling of trenches during day — nothing of interest happened. Casualties — 1 killed (rifle bullet) No. 5440. L/Cpl. J. Hutton B. Coy. This N.C.O. was buried in same place as P. Sinclair & P. McGall — on morning of 7th. Relieved by 1 R. Scots 6.15 p.m. Relief completed by 12.30 a.m. 7th with 1 Casualty — Wounded No. 6549. Dmr. J. McDonald B. Coy (S.B) During two days Bn. occupied trenches quantities of wire (entanglemen.) - revetments, sandbags &c were taken down. It was distressing to find in one trench that the rifle racks previously erected by us had been torn down & used for firewood by our relieving battalion. Fine — Wet later. Cold.	

	1/2/15	2/2	3/2	4/2	5/2	6/2	7/2	8/2	9/2	10/2	
Effective Strength	22,671	15	40	12	9	4	23	3	9		
BOESCHEPE	1	39									
WAR ESTAB:	31,976	15	42	12	9	4	23	3	9		
To Complete	8,266	+ 2									
Hospl {Wounded	1	15									2/Lt Walker
{Sick	3	144									H Anderson, Capt. Macdonald, Campbell
Base & Comd	4										S. Gibson, Lt Phillips 42 off servants
attached	7										
Rationed	22,671	15	40	12	9						
Strength	27,973										

2nd Battalion The Queen's Own Cameron Highlanders.

8/79th

Hour, Date, and Place	Summary of Events and Information	Remarks and References to Appendices
DICKEBUSCH 7th Feb. Sunday 1915	Remained in Billets. [Battn. sent by Coys: to new baths in brewery ¾ m. along road towards YPRES. — Day spent in resting & cleaning up. Bright & clear — rained at night]	

2nd Battalion The Queen's Own Cameron Highlanders.

8/79th

Hour, Date, and Place	Summary of Events and Information	Remarks and References to Appendices
DICKEBUSCH TRENCHES @ BRASSERIE 8th February Mon 1915	Remained in billets until 5.15 pm when C. Coy moved out to relieve R. Scots in BRASSERIE Section followed by B & A. @ 15 minutes interval. D took over BRASSERIE itself & remained in support. — [Situation B on right, A on left, C in close support in dug-outs (less one platoon in No 1 trench on right of B) & D in support @ BRASSERIE. H.Q. at BRASSERIE.] On marching out of billets No 8281 Pte W. Robertson B Coy. accidentally shot himself in ankle. Relief completed about 10 pm with one casualty No. 9315 Pte N. Crisp C. Coy. wounded. Work on improving trenches commenced at once & continued until dawn on 9th. Wire entanglement put out under R.E. supervision on R. of Section filling existing gaps between that & left of Right (WERTRAAT) portion of line. Trench mortar emplacement also constructed. Wet - Cold	

2nd Battalion The Queen's Own Cameron Highlanders.

2/79th

Hour, Date, and Place	Summary of Events and Information	Remarks and References to Appendices
TRENCHES @ BRASSERIE 9th Feb: Tues 1915	Occupied trenches. Enemy shelled BOIS CARRÉ (centre of our section) and our two right trenches without doing any material damage. One Casualty – Killed – [Shell wound] No. 9184 Pte T. Pace C. Coy. This man was buried on 10th in corner of field on N. side of road running W. from BRASSERIE & about 300 x from it. The morning was misty so much work was done by half D. Coy in making material for trenches. Later it cleared & enemy's Aeroplanes appeared. Later as on previous occasions all material in hand was carried down to trenches & used for improving & repairing damage. 2/Lt A.L. COLLIER (3/CH) joined & reported for duty – was posted to A Coy. Fine Clear. Cold.	

2nd Battalion The Queen's Own Cameron Highlanders.

8/79th

HOUR, DATE, AND PLACE	SUMMARY OF EVENTS AND INFORMATION	REMARKS AND REFERENCES TO APPENDICES
TRENCHES @ BRASSERIE to Huts MILLE KAPELLE. 10th Feb. Wed. 1915	Occupied trenches until relieved by 4/K.R.R.C. at 7.30 p.m. [Relief completed at 11 p.m. except A. Coy who owing to some mistake were not entirely relieved & did not get back to billets until very late.] One man accidentally wounded himself coming out of trenches. No. 7920. L/C. H. ERNST. C. Coy. During day Enemy's Aeroplane active [Two Bombs were dropped in vicinity of BRASSERIE. No damage done.] Shell fire on BOIS CARRÉ and on ELZENWALLE continued. Several hits obtained on houses in village.] Work by RE on right of line on night 9/10th entirely suspended owing to activity on Enemy's part - who threw up flares & by their light opened M.G. & rifle fire on working parties. Colt - Somerlain	

2nd Battalion The Queen's Own Cameron Highlanders.

2/79th

HOUR, DATE, AND PLACE	SUMMARY OF EVENTS AND INFORMATION	REMARKS AND REFERENCES TO APPENDICES
HILLE-KAPELLE to RENINGHELST 11th Feb. Thurs. 1915	At 11 am Bn. marched to Reserve Area [& took up billets in huts] at ZEVECOTEN ([RENINGHELST) officers in inns & farm cottages in neighbourhood.	Fine Cold.

2nd Battalion The Queen's Own Cameron Highlanders.

HOUR, DATE, AND PLACE	SUMMARY OF EVENTS AND INFORMATION	REMARKS AND REFERENCES TO APPENDICES
RENINGHELST 12th Feb. Friday 1915	Remained in billets. Baths allotted to Bn. for the day - men getting a complete change of under-clothing in exchange for dirty things. Ground in vicinity of huts in very muddy state, efforts made to improve approaches by cutting & laying fascine roads. Cold — Some rain	

2nd Battalion The Queen's Own Cameron Highlanders.

7/9th

HOUR, DATE, AND PLACE	SUMMARY OF EVENTS AND INFORMATION	REMARKS AND REFERENCES TO APPENDICES
RENINGHELST 13th Feb. Sat 1915	Remained in billets — some work done in improving approaches to huts. Heavy rain in morning fine later v. cold. 2/Lt. J.D. McLeod joined for duty & was posted to A Coy.	

	Off	OR	a.	LD	HD	P	MG	AR	2U	B	
Effective Strength	24	655	15	39	12	9	4	23	3	9	
Bon chefs	1	37									+ Inclusion M.O. & Chaplain
War Establishment	31	976	15	42	12	9	4	23	4	9	
To Complete	6	257	✓	3	✓	✓	✓	1ˣ	✓		ˣ Mess Cart
Sick	2	185									
Base & Comm		19									
Attached		7									
Rations	24	672	15	39	12	9					
Strength	27	844									

2nd Battalion The Queen's Own Cameron Highlanders.

7/79th

Hour, Date, and Place	Summary of Events and Information	Remarks and References to Appendices
RENINGHELST to VOORMEZEELE 14th Feb Sunday 1915	Remained in billets till 6 pm. when orders were received to 81 Bde to stand by to move to DICKEBUSCH in support of 82nd Bde holding dept section (8th E201) [At 7.15 Bn. marched independently and] on arrival at DICKEBUSCH at 8.45 pm. orders were received to move on to VOORMEZEELE. Bn. arrived there at 9.30 and remained until 7. am 15th when two Coys B & C went to CHATEAU — KRUISSTRAATHOEK — and two A & D to DICKEBUSCH. The support was not required. [Cause of alarm the Enemy attacked & took three trenches on right of 28th Div. and one trench on left of 27th Div. Counter attacks subsequently re-took these trenches. During night & especially from 3 to 4 am 15th when final counter-attacks were carried out very heavy bombardment by our Arty. took place first on our trenches re-occupied by enemy, & later on enemy's support trenches] Wounded [3/6107 Pte. McClure B. Coy.] Very Wet. Cold	

2nd Battalion The Queen's Own Cameron Highlanders.

Hour, Date, and Place	Summary of Events and Information	Remarks and References to Appendices
DICKEBUSCH 15th Feb. Monday 1915 South	Bn. returned from VOORMEZEELE two Coys A & D to DICKEBUSCH with HQ & two B & C to CHATEAU - KRUISSTRAATHOEK - No developments during day. At 8 pm Bn. moved out and took over right portion of Left Section of Trenches from R.I. Fusiliers (82nd Bde) H.Q. were established in BUS HOUSE (name derived from two broken motor buses on VOORMEZEELE - ST ELOI Road) A & D occupied left and right portion of front respectively, B Coy in close support in trenches on right of road between BUS House and "The Mound" - ST ELOI, & C in support in VOORMEZEELE - At 9 pm relief was suspended until 10.15 owing to heavy firing North of ST ELOI. relief finally completed about 11:30. At 9.20 owing to sudden very heavy burst of firing on our left the S.O.S. signal was sent to Arty who quickly responded until firing diminished. Casualties - Killed 1 Major P.T.C. Baird [9.30.pm from shell wound in throat received at crossroads by Church in VOORMEZEELE.] 3 Wounded [No. 8090 Pte J. Steele C. Coy. " 9067 L/Cpl. W. Humble C " " 7910 L/Cpl J. Crichton B "] Cold Wet	2/79a

2nd Battalion The Queen's Own Cameron Highlanders.

2/79th

Hour, Date, and Place	Summary of Events and Information	Remarks and References to Appendices
TRENCHES (BUS-HOUSE) to DICKEBUSCH 16th Feb: Tues 1915	Battn occupied Trenches until the evening when they were relieved by 1/R. Scots. [In the morning before dawn B & C changed places, the former going in to VOORMEZEELE & the latter to support trench.] Casualties during 24 hrs. Killed 2 No. 15950 Pte J. Connell A. Coy " 8575 " T. Hall A. " Wounded - No. 7864 Pte D. Alexander D. Coy " 4848 " J. Hanna D. " " 5929 " M. Hamilton C. " ⊖ " 9806 " T. Forrest A. " ✗ ⊖ Died of wounds ✗ Died of wounds in Clearing Hospl 19/2/15 On relief H.Q., B & C went to Dickebusch A & D to Chateau - KRUISSTRAAT HOEK Cold - wet.	

2nd Battalion The Queen's Own Cameron Highlanders.

17

N/79th

Hour, Date, and Place	Summary of Events and Information	Remarks and References to Appendices
DICKEBUSCH 17th Feb. Wed 1915	Bn. remained in billets until 7pm when H.Q. moved to CHATEAU KRUISSTRAATHOEK — and joined A & D Coys — B & C going to VOORMEZEELE — This move was occasioned by word coming through from 28th Divn that Germans had re-occupied two of our trenches. Nothing happened during night and early next morning H.Q. & B.C. moved back to Dickebusch. Funeral of Maj. Baird took place at 8 a.m — grave in field E of Church. DICKEBUSCH.	Wet — Cold

2nd Battalion The Queen's Own Cameron Highlanders.

Hour, Date, and Place	Summary of Events and Information	Remarks and References to Appendices
DICKEBUSCH & TRENCHES (BUS-HOUSE) 18th Feb. Thurs 1915	A quiet day spent in Billets except at 9 am when enemy sent some shells over CHATEAU, one burst over a barn occupied by some of A. Coy casualty following Casualties — Killed) 8295 Pte D. Johnstone H Wounded (Died of Wounds) 8199 " F. Hay. A. Wounded 3 6678 " C. Bleasdale A. 8695 L/Cpl J. Ross A S/11153 Pte J. Anderson. A. Bn. relieved 1/R. Scots. in Trenches a 8-20 pm B + C in fire trenches – B on left – A in support trench behind Mound (S.9) D in VOORMEZEELE Casualties — Wounded (Died of wounds) No. 8576 Sgt Munro C. Coy Wounded " 7778 Pte Chalmers B. No 9213 Pte G. Begbie B Coy accidentally shot himself in hand in billets Cold – Dry. E wind	

2nd Battalion The Queen's Own Cameron Highlanders.

Hour, Date, and Place	Summary of Events and Information	Remarks and References to Appendices
TRENCHES (BUS-HOUSE) 19th Feb: Friday 1915	Bn. occupied trenches - A quiet day. At about 8 pm A Coy relieved B and D relieved C. B & C moving to support trench and VOORMEZEELE respectively. Casualties. Killed 4 Wounded 1 (No 9806 Pte T. Forrel A Coy wounded on 16th inst. reported from Hospl died of wounds)	No. 5496 Sgt A. McGillevray B.Coy " 4416 Pte J. McDonald B. " " 8829 " T. Donnelley C. " " 8890 " A. Chisholm B. " No. 8344 " J. McKinnon D "

2nd Battalion The Queen's Own Cameron Highlanders.

7/79th

Hour, Date, and Place	Summary of Events and Information	Remarks and References to Appendices
TRENCHES (BUS-HOUSE) to DICKEBUSCH 20th Feb. Sat. 1915	Bn occupied trenches during day A & D in fire trenches - A on left. B in support trench and C at VOORMEZEELE. At 4 pm very heavy firing was heard from N. which proved later to be an attack Hazebrouck by Germans & counter attack by 27th Divn on trenches N. of Canal & due E. of YPRES. [This firing died away at dusk - but broke out again about 9 pm & was continued until morning of 21st.] Bn was relieved by 1/R.Scots at 8 pm relief completed without casualties in Bn: at 11 pm with exception of 1 trench occupied by platoon of A. R.Scots approaching gave indication of their presence & enemy opened heavy fire causing several casualties in their ranks and delaying relief of this portion until 2 am 21st. Casualties during day. Killed - Lt R.A.H. Densmore. D.Coy No.8964 Pte H. Owens A wounded No.8353 " W. Budge A	

Wet - Cold.

	M.O.	O.R.	C	LD	ND	P	M.G.	4W	2W	B	
Effective Strength	21*	600	15	38	12	9	4	21	3	9	* Includes M.O. & Chaplain
Attached	2*	36									Lt Thomson, 2 Lt MacFadyen
War Estab	31*	976	15	42	12	9	4	21	4	9	* Mess Cart
To complete	8*	340	ʘ	4	ʘ	ʘ	ʘ	ʘ	ʘ	ʘ	
Sick	2*	205									Capt Maclean, Capt MacDonald
Base & Lines		17									
Attached		7									
Battalion	21	617	15	38	12	9					
Strength	25	858									

2nd Battalion The Queen's Own Cameron Highlanders.

Hour, Date, and Place	Summary of Events and Information	Remarks and References to Appendices
DICKEBUSCH 21st Feb. Sunday 1915	Bn. remained in billets during day. At 3.30 pm funeral of Lt Dawson & Lt Stirling (A&SH) was held in field E. Church in DICKEBUSCH - location of grave about 100ˣ from church close to VIERSTRAAT road. Cold - Fine.	

2nd Battalion The Queen's Own Cameron Highlanders.

2/79th

Hour, Date, and Place	Summary of Events and Information	Remarks and References to Appendices
DICKEBUSCH to TRENCHES (BUS-HOUSE) 22nd Feb. Monday 1915	Bn. remained in billets until 5.30 pm when relief of 1/R. Scots in Trenches commenced. [All coys washed at Brewery 3/4 m. along YPRES Road.] Relief of Trenches. B Coy took over left of line, C. right of line, D in Support Trenches, A. in Reserve @ VOORMEZEELE. Relief completed 9.45 pm. Enemy fairly quiet on our front though considerable firing was heard on N. (28th Divn.) The night was very foggy which hid moon & assisted relief. Trenches on the whole reported in very bad state in many cases worse than when last handed over by us. Casualty — Wounded No. 7724 Pte P. Robertson B. Coy (Self inflicted)	Cold – Wet – Foggy from 4.30 pm onwards

2nd Battalion The Queen's Own Cameron Highlanders.

2/79th

DATE, AND PLACE	SUMMARY OF EVENTS AND INFORMATION	REMARKS AND REFERENCES TO APPENDICES
TRENCHES (BUS-HOUSE) 23rd Feb. Thursday 1915	Work in Trenches continued - Coys in support filling & taking to trenches sandbags brought to St E201 by Reserve Coy. At 1 am a message came to Bn. Hqrs from MOUND (S.13) to effect that three officers & some men had been wounded at No 16. Trench - [On investigation facts appeared as follows.] An orderly - Pte McKellar - approaching the trench was shot - Lt Nicholson & Sgt McIver went to his assistance & both were hit - A messenger then went from No 17 to fetch a stretcher party - passed Lt Davidson on the way - who immediately came down to No 16 to render assistance he remained with Nicholson lying beside him till Capt Fraser from S.13 arrived with stretcher - As Nicholson was being put on stretcher both Fraser & Davidson were hit - the former killed outright - Word was then telephoned up from 17. & further stretchers were sent & dead & wounded carried to Aid Post. Lt Nicholson died about an hour later. It is practically certain that all the shots came from Sap-head as shown in sketch in margin. Day quiet - some shelling - At 8pm Coys in support & Reserve relieved front line. Casualties Killed - Capt P.W.N. FRASER. D.S.O. B.Coy. No 8878 Pte J CAMERON C Coy " 8909 " J Sullivan " " 8752 " A McKellar A " " 869 " J Syme B " Died of wounds Lt W.D. NICHOLSON B Coy Wounded - Lt D.G. DAVIDSON (M.Gun) 3/29.9 Sgt H. McIVER. A Coy, 8094 Pte G MANSFIELD B Coy 3/11311 Pte S. DOCHERTY B Coy, 7800 Pte J. KAY C Coy, 8904 Pte J WRIGHT C Coy, 5 Wet - V. Cold.	Bus-House / Ypres / Mound / Capt Fraser / No 17 / Sap Head Source of Fire / German Parallel / X = Place where officers & men were hit

2nd Battalion The Queen's Own Cameron Highlanders.

Hour, Date, and Place	Summary of Events and Information	Remarks and References to Appendices
TRENCHES (BUS-HOUSE) to DICKEBUSCH. 24th February Wed 1915	Bn. occupied trenches during day until relieved by 1/R. Scots @ 7 pm relief completed at 9.30 pm. Moon very bright. Casualties during relief 4 men hit coming out of S.P. Day buried very wet and cold after frosty night. G.O.C. 1 Bde visited Bn H.Q. early in the morning. Work in trenches during darkness continued & considerable improvement effected. Casualties Wounded 5 No. 8763 Pte A. McIntosh D. Coy. " 8216 " J. McIntyre D " " 8005 " R. Gourley D " " 8559 LCpl J. Reid D " " 8752 Pte J. Clarke D " Cold & v. wet. Pte Syme was buried in rear of his trench No 18. S. of St Eloi Ptes Cameron & Sullivan were buried @ VOORMEZEELE B & C coys moved to Chateau on relief and A & D to Dickebusch.	

2nd Battalion The Queen's Own Cameron Highlanders.

7/79th

Hour, Date, and Place	Summary of Events and Information	Remarks and References to Appendices
DICKEBUSCH 25th Feb. Thurs. 1915	Bn. Remained in Billets - A & D. Coys. in DICKEBUSCH - B & C at Chateau. At 3 pm funeral of Capt. W.N. Fraser, Lt. W.D. Nicholson, Pte. McKellar, and one officer & two men A&SH. took place in field next Church - The graves were dug in same place as Lt. Dunsmure's - The piece of ground was enclosed by wire. At about 9.30 pm heavy firing was heard from line left of St. ELOI. but Bn. was not turned out. Dry & Cold.	

2nd Battalion The Queen's Own Cameron Highlanders.

2/79th

Hour, Date, and Place	Summary of Events and Information	Remarks and References to Appendices
DICKEBUSCH to TRENCHES (BUS-HOUSE) 26th Feb. Friday 1915	Remained in Billets [A & D at Dickebusch B & C @ Chateau] Bn. relieved R. Scots on right portion of left section S. & W. of St ELOI. C on right, B on left, A in support, D in VOORMEZEELE with 2 platoons R. Scots. Relief began 8.30 & was completed by 10.45 without casualties in Bn inspite of very bright moon. This lack of casualties points clearly to fact that French commanders lead their men well & have them well in hand. It has bee shewn over & over again that if Enemy is at all awake, any slackness in allowing noise or lights inevitably brings disaster & not only to the party relieving, but to those relieved. 2/Lt H.R Tollemache joined from 3/Battn, Posted to A.Coy Bright clear day. Frost.	

2nd Battalion The Queen's Own Cameron Highlanders.

2/79th

Gale & Polden, Ltd., Printers, Aldershot. 7,657-11.

Hour, Date, and Place	Summary of Events and Information	Remarks and References to Appendices
TRENCHES (Bus - HOUSE) to RENINGHELST 27th Feb. Saturday 1915	Bn. occupied trenches as taken over on 26th Enemy quiet in front of our trenches. A Coy in Support trench dug in three men on right of their trench who were able to effect some sniping during day. They reported having shot a German in enemy's trench in front of Trench 15. About 3.30 pm Enemy shelled trenches on our right flank our guns retaliating on theirs. Firing continued until dusk. At 8.30 pm Bn was relieved by 4/R.Bde. (no casualties during relief) and Coys] moved [independently] to [Huts at] RENINGHELST [halting at MILLE KAPELLE for tea which had been prepared there - last Coy arrived in Huts at 1.30 am 28th]	
	[Casualties during day.	
	Killed [No. 9254 a/Sgt. T. Ross. C Coy. The body was buried in rear of trenches]	
	Wounded [No. 8771. Pte Duff C Coy	
	" 6746 " Scott C. "	
	" 9290 " McDonald C. "]	
	Rain Very Cold.	

	Off	O Rank	Chargers	L.D.	H.D.	Mule	M.G.	W.W.	2 W.	D.	Remarks
Effective Strength	29x	539	15	37	12	9	4	21	4	9	Includes MO & Chaplain
Boeschepe	1x	28									Lt Thomson
War Estab't	31	916	15	42	12	9	4	21	4	9	
To complete	11	409	✓	5	✓	✓	✓	✓	✓	✓	
Sick	1x	207									Lt Macfadyen
Base Wounded		24									
Attached		7									
Ration	20	546									
Strength	22	798									

A D McL Capt Adjt

2nd Battalion The Queen's Own Cameron Highlanders.

7/79th

Hour, Date, and Place	Summary of Events and Information	Remarks and References to Appendices
RENINGHELST 25th Feb. Sunday 1915	Bn. remained in Billets in Huts. Coys. occupying same huts as before. Found no improvement since last occupation. Ground in vicinity still in a shocking state & no paths made. No arrangements at all for washing, for which there is no excuse — as it is the one thing that is essential when Bn. returns from trenches and have to wait some days before their turn comes for use of Hot Baths. Although RENINGHELST is a fair sized town the officers are billeted in the filthiest hovels imaginable, where the greatest difficulty is experienced in procuring cooking & washing facilities. Divisional & Brigade Staffs, on the other hand, are extremely comfortably housed. 2/Lt. R.R. McIntosh 3/Bn. joined & posted to B Coy. 70 men joined. Cold – frost. E. wind	

81st Inf.Bde.
27th Div.

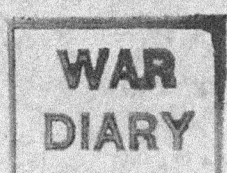

2nd BATTN. THE QUEEN'S OWN CAMERON HIGHLANDERS.

M A R C H

1 9 1 5

2nd Battalion The Queen's Own Cameron Highlanders.

Hour, Date, and Place	Summary of Events and Information	Remarks and References to Appendices
RENINGHELST 1st March Monday 1915	Remained in Billets. [50 men in two reliefs. A Coy in morning - B in afternoon constructed "Knife rest" wire entanglements. Remainder worked on improving approaches to huts.] At 10.0 am orders received to stand by to support 80th Bde. if required - these orders subsequently cancelled at 3 pm. G.O.C. Bde. inspected draft which arrived on 28th ultimo. Instruction of Officers & N.C.O. men in bomb throwing continued (2/Lt. Mills) Rain & snow storm accompanied by thunder & lightning — Cold (No. 8929. Pte M. Hamilton C Coy. wounded on 16th Feb. reported from Hospt. died of wounds)	

2nd Battalion The Queen's Own Cameron Highlanders.

Hour, Date, and Place	Summary of Events and Information	Remarks and References to Appendices
RENINGHELST 2nd March. Tues. 1915	Remained in Billets. Fatigue parties working on "Knife rest" wire entanglements unable to continue owing to lack of tools & material. Instruction in Bomb throwing to party of 8 men continued — Instruction commenced to party of 16 men in Sapping. At 6.30pm. Battn and Gloucesters ordered to stand by during night — to support 80th Bde if required — not however called on. 2nd Lt Macleod & 6635 L/Cpl Stewart proceeded to St OMER for Machine Gun Course. Fine — Cold.	

2nd Battalion The Queen's Own Cameron Highlanders.

Hour, Date, and Place	Summary of Events and Information	Remarks and References to Appendices
RENINGHELST 3rd March Wed. 1915	Remained in billets - continued to work on "Knife rest". Instruction continued in Sapping & bomb throwing - which latter party was increased to two men per platoon. Battalion had use of baths for day all men washed & obtained change of clothing. Lt A Fowler took over temp. the duties of Staff Capt. T. Bde. Very wet & cold.	Fatigue parties

2nd Battalion The Queen's Own Cameron Highlanders.

Hour, Date, and Place	Summary of Events and Information	Remarks and References to Appendices
RENINGHELST 4th March Thursday 1915	Remained in billets. Instruction continued in sapping & bomb-throwing. Work also continued on making "knife rests".	
	Fine - warmer - no sun	

2nd Battalion The Queen's Own Cameron Highlanders.

Hour, Date, and Place	Summary of Events and Information	Remarks and References to Appendices
RENINGHELST to DICKEBUSCH 5th March. Friday 1915	At 5.40 p.m. Battn with A&SH marched to DICKEBUSCH. Bn. billeted & Bn. H.Q. & B Coy at HALEBLAST Corner, A Coy in DICKEBUSCH, C & D Coys in farms on VIERSTRAAT Road. R. Scots & Gloucesters took over Right Section of trenches from 82nd Bde. A&SH in close support – 1 Coy ELZENWALLE – remainder at HALEBLAST Corner (!) Now settled, though details of scheme not yet worked out, that 81 Bde take over right section of trenches permanently, 80th & 82nd being responsible for left section (S. OS). 81st Bde to be augmented by 9th R. Scots & 9th A. & S.H. – the two territorial units to have instruction in trench fighting before taking their turn as Bns. in the front line. DRY – COLD	

	Offrs	O.R.	Chargd	LD	HD	Pack	MG	WH	2W	Bicycles	
Effective Strength BOESCHEPE	22 ✓	593 33	15	40	12	9	4	21	4	9	x Includes H.Q. Chaplain & Lt MacLeod @ St Omar
WAR ESTABLISHMT	31	976	15	62	12	9	4	21	9	9	
To Complete	9	350	✓	2	✓	✓	✓	✓	✓	✓	
Sick	2x	181									x Capt MacLean & Lt Macfadyen
Base & Command		30									
Attached		7									
Rationed Strength	22 24	600 837 *	15	40	12	9					* Excludes O.R. Sgt.

2nd Battalion The Queen's Own Cameron Highlanders.

Hour, Date, and Place	Summary of Events and Information	Remarks and References to Appendices
DICKEBUSCH 6th March Saturday 1915	Bn. remained in billets occupied the previous night. Units informed that trenches 21 - 15 had been vacated (temporarily) in the morning to allow the combined artillery to shell enemy's trenches opposite. Shelling commenced at 12 noon & continued slowly until dusk with little reply from enemy's guns. Reported that much damage was done to enemy's parapets. Trenches were again reoccupied at dusk without interference.	
7 pm	D. Coy ordered to stand by ready to turn out at moments notice & proceed to cross roads in rear of BRASSERIE. Nothing happened.	
		Much rain - misty & cold

2nd Battalion The Queen's Own Cameron Highlanders.

Hour, Date, and Place	Summary of Events and Information	Remarks and References to Appendices
DICKEBUSCH to TRENCHES (BRASSERIE) 7th Mar. Sunday 1915	Bn. remained in billets during day. At 9.30 a.m. B. Coy. at HALEBAST corner reported they had moved from billet to open ground about 1000 yds W. as enemy were shelling the cross-roads & neighbourhood. Several Argylls were hit & some transport. About 5.30 pm Enemy again shelled the place one man was hit. Casualty - wounded No. 8196 Pte R. Pryde A. Coy. At 7.0 pm Bn. relieved 1 R. Scots in right sector of right section. A & C. Coys occupied fire trenches on left & right respectively, D in Support trenches, & B. in reserve at BRASSERIE with Bn. H.q. No casualties during relief. Relief completed about 11 pm. A party of 8 men & a Cpl. under Sgt Maj. E. Fraser were organized as Snipers & given a roving commission to observe, and to effect as much damage on enemy by sniping as possible. The trenches in left section had again been vacated to allow our guns to fire on enemy's fire trenches. At dusk these trenches were reported safely re-occupied. Wet and cold.	

2nd Battalion The Queen's Own Cameron Highlanders.

Hour, Date, and Place	Summary of Events and Information	Remarks and References to Appendices

TRENCHES (BRASSERIE) 8th March Monday 1915	Bn. occupied trenches as taken over on previous night. Nothing of special interest occurred during day. Enemy quiet and little artillery fire observed.
	
	At 9.5pm Two platoons 9th A.&S.H. arrived from hut shelters (a Reserve Hill) to be attached to Coys: in trenches for instruction. A quantity of material was carried by night to trenches by the Coy in Reserve & used for repairing. A dug-out in rear of BRASSERIE begun on a former occasion was completed. R.E. Assistance was rendered to the trench commanders in some cases.
	
	Casualties during day
	Wounded — {No. 8757 Pte K. McKenzie C. Coy
	          " 6375 L/Cpl J. Davie C. "
	          " 5775 Pte J. Aitken A. "
	These men were shot accidentally by another man in the same trench.
	No. 8020 Pte H. Young C.Coy reported having accidentally shot himself at BOESCHEPE
	
	Windy & intensely cold.	

2nd Battalion The Queen's Own Cameron Highlanders.

Hour, Date, and Place	Summary of Events and Information	Remarks and References to Appendices
TRENCHES (BRASSERIE) to DICKEBUSCH 9th March Tues. 1915	Bn. occupied trenches during day. At 7.30 pm. relief by 1/Royal Scots commenced which was not completed until 11.30 pm. No casualties during relief. From 6 am until 7 pm our Artillery shelled enemy's trenches as on 6th & 7th, our infantry vacating trenches during day. Much damage reported as being done. On relief A. Coy moved to ELZENWALLE B, C, D, M. Gun & H.Qrs. to DICKEBUSCH. 2 Platoons 9th Argylls relieved at same time & returned to Huts at ROSEN HILL. Casualties during day Killed No. 9877. Pte W. Hogg D. Coy Wounded " S/12409 " J. McAlpine A. " Fine - frost & very cold.	

2nd Battalion The Queen's Own Cameron Highlanders.

Hour, Date, and Place	Summary of Events and Information	Remarks and References to Appendices
DICKEBUSCH 10th March Wed. 1915	Bn. remained in Billets in close support in DICKEBUSCH — A. Coy at ELZENWALLE. Chaplain went out to BRASSERIE to conduct funeral of Pte Hogg. who was buried in same enclosure as Pte Pace (see 9th Feb.)	Wet — Cold.

2nd Battalion The Queen's Own Cameron Highlanders.

Hour, Date, and Place	Summary of Events and Information	Remarks and References to Appendices
DICKEBUSCH to TRENCHES (BRASSERIE) 11th March Thurs. 1915	Remained in billets until 8 pm when Bn. relieved 1/R. Scots. During day heavy artillery fire directed on St ELOI trenches. Relief completed about midnight, no casualties. B & D Coys held fire trenches left & right respectively, C in support trench & A in reserve at BRASSERIE. Fine & warmer.	

2nd Battalion The Queen's Own Cameron Highlanders.

Hour, Date, and Place	Summary of Events and Information	Remarks and References to Appendices
TRENCHES (BRASSERIE) 12th March, Friday 1915	Bn. occupied Trenches. Orders received that at 7·30am a heavy burst of rifle fire was to commence on enemy's trenches simultaneously with bombardment of HOLLANDSCHESCHUUR FARM by our artillery – owing to heavy mist this was postponed until 3pm when it took place. Considerable damage done to enemy's parapets & a certain amount to own from their reply. Object of manoeuvre to contain them & prevent their withdrawing their reserves to line being attacked by 3rd Divn. South of WYTCHAETE – General effect of fire to make trench occupiers opposite a bit jumpy & extra watchful – [Unofficial news came in that 3rd Divn attack had been unsuccessful.]	
✗ Buried on 13th at BRASSERIE	Casualties – Killed No 9031 Pte D. Cameron D. Coy " 7459 A. Fleming D. " " 7148 A. Bryce B. " " 7902 A. Rennie D. " Wounded No. 5113 Pte A Cameron D. Coy " 8860 " J. McGinn D. " " 8965 " J. McFarlane C. " " 9224 " A. Hogarth B. " " 8932 " J. McAulay B. " " S/13092 " S. Young B. " " 7752 L.Cpl W. Walker B. "	
	Two Platoons 9th R. Scots attached for instn. one man was wounded. Misty – milder	

2nd Battalion The Queen's Own Cameron Highlanders.

Hour, Date, and Place	Summary of Events and Information	Remarks and References to Appendices
TRENCHES (BRASSERIE) to DICKEBUSCH 13th March Saturday 1915	Bn. held trenches until relieved by 1/R. Scots at 8.30 pm. Relief completed by midnight. At 4 am a repetition of "programme" carried out at 3.15 pm on Friday, was made with much the same effect - Enemy's fire very wild, many bullets dropping on VIERSTRAAT - BRASSERIE line. At 2.15 pm similar programme again carried out with same results. Casualties. Killed No. 9250 Pte D. Chalmers B. Coy. Wounded No 7124 Pte T. Auld D. Coy " 8806 " A. Campbell B. " ˣ Lt. A.Y.G. Thomson slightly wounded. B. Coy. Warmer & much drier Lt. G. Fowler returned from officiating Staff Capt. 77. Bde. Notification received of Commissions having been granted to C.S.M. K Cameron & J. Gifford	ˣ buried @ BRASSERIE 13/3/15.

	Off	O.R.	Chap.l	L.D	H.D	P	M.G.	4W	2W	Bicycle	
Effective Strength	ˣ23	605	15	37	12	9	4	21	4	9	ˣ Includes M.O. & Chaplain & ⁺Lt. McLeod @ St Omer
Boeschepe		23									
War Establishm't	ˣ31	976	15	42	12	9	4	21	4	9	
To Complete	8	268	✓	5	✓	✓	✓	✓	✓	✓	
Sick	1	173									⁺Lt. Macfadyen
Base & Command		39									
Attached		7									
Strength	24	820	15	37	12	9	4	21	4	9	

2nd Battalion The Queen's Own Cameron Highlanders.

Hour, Date, and Place	Summary of Events and Information	Remarks and References to Appendices
DICKEBUSCH to BRASSERIE (2nd line) 14th Mar Sunday 1915	Bn. occupied billets. At 5.15 pm fierce bombardment by German Artillery directed on Mound (St ELOI) *held by 2nd Bde* & VOORMEZEELE and on guns in front of DICKEBUSCH, which opened in reply. This was a prelude to German attack on Mound & neighbouring trenches at 7.15 pm which was successful. At 9 pm German Artillery ceased firing our guns however keeping it up all night on Mound & vicinity. At 7.30 pm orders received to move at once to new subsidiary line of trenches in rear of BRASSERIE. Bn. moved up & occupied this working all night at improving parapet. Casualties Wounded No. S/13310 Pte P. Divers A. Coy 5708 " D. Richardson C "	Lt. Steele A & S. H. buried at Dickebusch. Cold. dry.

2nd Battalion The Queen's Own Cameron Highlanders.

Hour, Date, and Place	Summary of Events and Information	Remarks and References to Appendices
BRASSERIE (2nd Line) to TRENCHES (BRASSERIE) 15th March Monday 1915	Bn. occupied Subsidiary line all day until 6.30 pm when relief of 1 R. Scots took place. Relief completed about 10 pm. One Coy 9th R. Scots arrived at 8 pm & were distributed between Coys. A & C Coys occupied left & right trenches, B in support trenches, D at Brasserie & KERSTRAAT. Information received that Counter-Attack on Mound ST ELOI by 80th & 82nd Bdes failed & that enemy still occupied it & surrounding trenches.	
Arrived @ Brasserie 16th	Casualties Killed No. 7416 Pte. J. Maitland D. Coy. Wounded No. 8693 Pte. J. Taylor B. Coy " 8694 Sgt. H. McDonald D " " S/14460 Pte. W. Stewart C " Misty - day.	

2nd Battalion The Queen's Own Cameron Highlanders.

Hour, Date, and Place	Summary of Events and Information	Remarks and References to Appendices
TRENCHES (BRASSERIE) 16th March, Tues. 1915	Bn. occupied trenches as taken over on 16th. Day was very misty which probably accounted for silence of artillery on both sides as compared with previous day or two. Some heavy bursts of fire were heard from N.E. & E. direction. At 7 p.m. a Coy 9th Argylls arrived & were sent to trenches in relief of Coy. 9th R. Scots.	
x buried @ Braserie on 16th	x Casualties killed No 9077 Pte F. Robertson C. Coy. Wounded, one man 9th Argylls. Misty Warm	

2nd Battalion The Queen's Own Cameron Highlanders.

Hour, Date, and Place	Summary of Events and Information	Remarks and References to Appendices
TRENCHES (BRASSERIE) 17th March - Wed. 1915	Bn. continued to occupy trenches. Very quiet day and night. No news of situation at St ELOI. After dark Coys. relieved each other. B & A exchanging & C & D C. coming to Brasserie. Casualties Wounded (died of wounds) No. 3/5644 Lt. J. Wallace C. Coy. Lt. L.R.M. Napier joined from Invergordon (he had been left in India for nucs of territorials). Misty - bright later - v. dark night 2Lt. Macleod, & L/Cpl Stewart rejoined from Machine Gun Course St Omer	

2nd Battalion The Queen's Own Cameron Highlanders.

Hour, Date, and Place	Summary of Events and Information	Remarks and References to Appendices
TRENCHES (BRASSERIE) 18th March Thurs. 1915	Bn. occupied trenches. Quiet day but misty which prevented any effective artillery fire. At 9. am the Chaplain - Mr Gilchrist - came out from Dickebusch to bury L.Cpl. Wallace C. Coy. who died of wounds previous day - Also a man of 9/A&SH. At 8 pm a Coy 9/A&SH relieved the Coy of same Bn. in the trenches - being split up as on former occasion. Casualties Wounded Capt A. Macduff 2Lt. J. Murray No S/13121. Pte J. Dromachie " 5592 " W Millar " 9100 " G. Kincaid and 2. 9th Argyll & Sutherland Highlanders. Misty - Mild.	D. Coy D. " D. " } accidentally self inflicted C. " B. "

2nd Battalion The Queen's Own Cameron Highlanders.

Hour, Date, and Place	Summary of Events and Information	Remarks and References to Appendices
TRENCHES (BRASSERIE) to ROSEN-HILL HUTS 19th March Friday 1915	Bn. occupied trenches during a quiet day. [At dawn the R.E. advanced depôt was moved from BRASSERIE to MIDDLE FARM in rear of BOIS CONFLUANT.] At 6 pm Bn. was relieved in trenches by 1st and 4th Gordon Highrs and at BRASSERIE by 4th Middlesex. These units formed part of 3rd Divn who took over greater part of right Section 27th Divn to enable it to shorten its line behind St ELOI, & strengthen 2nd & 3rd line of defences. Relief completed about 12 mn. No casualties. Coys. marched independently to billets in huts – distance 3½ miles. Heavy snow to 6.30 am; which cleared off & left a bright day but bitterly cold.	

2nd Battalion The Queen's Own Cameron Highlanders.

Hour, Date, and Place	Summary of Events and Information	Remarks and References to Appendices
ROSEN-HILL 20th March, Saturday 1915	Bn. occupied billets in huts at ROSEN-HILL. These were newly erected in a small copse on right hand side of ZEVECOTEN-LA CLYTTE road about 100x from road. They were solidly constructed of wood with waterproof felt covering to roof. Brushwood tracks had been made by former occupants — no cooking or washing arrangements were provided. In this respect the lack of Field Cookers is severely felt by the Battn* — repeatedly they would have proved of the utmost use. Limbered wagons are a poor substitute. In this connection it should be recorded that not only the two Supply Wagons, but also two out of four remaining wagons, have been taken by A.S.C. Great difficulty is experienced in transporting blankets & packs — which are not taken to trenches from billet to billet when the Bn is in the trenches. Fine — v. Cold.	
*Field Cookers eventually received on 30th March.		

	off.	O.R.	M.	LD	HO	P	MG	4W	2W	B	
Effective Strength	x23	653	15	39	12	9	4	21	4	9	x Inclus. M.O. & Chaplain
On charge		31									
War Estd	x31	976	15	42	12	9	4	21	4	9	
To Complete	8	312	✓	3	✓	✓	✓	✓	✓	✓	
Sick	+1	183									+Lt. Macfadyen
Bruised & wounded		2									
Attached		7									
Strength	24	869	15	39	12	9	4	21	4	9	

No. 8482 Pte. McLaney C. Coy went to St Omer for Machine Gun course.

2nd Battalion The Queen's Own Cameron Highlanders.

Hour, Date, and Place	Summary of Events and Information	Remarks and References to Appendices
ROSEN HILL 21st March Sunday 1915	Bn. remained in billets in huts. At 7.50 pm 150 men to KRUISSTRAATHOEK to dig on second line trenches between VOORMEZEELE & KRUISSTRAATHOEK - party returned at 3 am 22nd. Draft of 50 men arrived from Invergordon. Sapping party under instruction increased to 1. N.C.O. & 32 men. Bright - Warmer	A & B Coys marched with R.E. material

2nd Battalion The Queen's Own Cameron Highlanders.

Hour, Date, and Place	Summary of Events and Information	Remarks and References to Appendices
ROSEN-HILL 22nd March Monday 1915	Bn. remained in billets in huts. Opportunity taken to exercise men in platoon drill & the last draft in bayonet fighting & musketry. Regtl Sappers & Bomb throwers were also taken out for instruction. A seven foot Catapult was received for throwing bombs & with slight alteration might prove of some value. It is rather heavy & cumbersome. 100 men B & C. Coys dug on 2nd line behind VOORMEZEELE from 5pm to 2am 23rd. Lt A Fowler again took over duties Staff Capt M. Bde. Bright — warmer.	

2nd Battalion The Queen's Own Cameron Highlanders.

Hour, Date, and Place	Summary of Events and Information	Remarks and References to Appendices

ROSEN-HILL to CANADA-HUTS (DICKEBUSCH) 23rd March–Tuesday 1915	Bn. remained in ROSEN-HILL HUTS until 4.30 pm. when it moved to CANADA-HUTS about 300 yds N.W. HALEBAST cross road. At 6 pm. party of 300 men C, D & A Coys marched to point in rear of St ELOI and dug trenches under direction of R.E.
	
	2/Lt. G. Cadenhead 3rd Bn. joined & was posted to D. Coy.
	
	Casualties during digging
	Wounded [No 1186 L/Cpl. S. Hatton C. Coy.
	        " 8866 Pte G. Berry C. "
	        " 9260 " M. Grant C. "
	        S/14432 " G. Young C. "]
	
	Fine - mild - rain towards evening.	

2nd Battalion The Queen's Own Cameron Highlanders.

Hour, Date, and Place	Summary of Events and Information	Remarks and References to Appendices
CANADA-HUTS 24th March-Wed. 1915	Bn. remained in billets in huts. At 10 pm. Coys. (500 mm) moved independently to cross roads 500 yds N. of BRASSERIE picking up pickets at R.E. Park DICKEBUSCH. On arrival at rendezvous Coys were met by guides & taken to portion of G.H.Q. line of trenches where work of digging & wiring was continued. Work ceased at 3.30 a.m. 25th & Coys returned independently to huts. Casualty: Wounded No. 5465 Pte H Tait D. Coy. Fine morning heavy rain later - fine night cold by day - warmer @ night.	

2nd Battalion The Queen's Own Cameron Highlanders.

Hour, Date, and Place	Summary of Events and Information	Remarks and References to Appendices
CANADA - HUTS. 25th March Thursday 1915	Bn. remained in huts. Working parties on G.H.Q. line of trenches in two reliefs - First A & B Coys 200 men at 6.30 pm - Second C & D Coys 200 men at 11 pm.	Rained all day until about 5.30 pm. Very cold

2nd Battalion The Queen's Own Cameron Highlanders.

Hour, Date, and Place	Summary of Events and Information	Remarks and References to Appendices
CANADA - HUTS 26th March Friday 1915	Bn. occupied huts. Orders received that Battn & 1/A&SH. were temp: attached to 82nd Bde. who were reserve to 3rd Divn. occupying trenches. During night 26th-27th heavy firing both rifle & artillery was heard in direction of St ELOI & N. of that place. Firing continuous all night till dawn. Wet & very cold.	

2nd Battalion The Queen's Own Cameron Highlanders.

Hour, Date, and Place	Summary of Events and Information	Remarks and References to Appendices
CANAD- HUTS 27th March Sat 1915	Bn. remained in billets in huts; continuing to be temp: attached to 82nd Bde. who were in reserve to 3rd Divn in trenches. At 3 pm. 2nd in Command, M.Gun & bomb throwing officers, five Coy officers and 12 NCOs left by motor bus from ZOVECOTEN for YPRES to visit trenches E of that place which Bn. would occupy when 27th Divn relieved the French. Bright sun - Intensely cold wind.	

	Off	O.R.	Ch.	L.D	H.D.	P.	M.4	4.W	2.W	Light	
Effective Strength	ˣ24	695	15	39	12	9	4	21	⁺7	9	ˣ Inclusn M.O. & Chaplain
War Establishment	ˣ31	976	15	42	12	9	4	21	⁺7	9	⁺ Increase 3 hand carts.
To Complete	7	278	✓	3	✓	✓	✓	✓	✓	✓	
Sick in Hospl	1	217									°Lt. Macfadyen
Base & Comm.		2									
Attached		7									
Strength	25	917	15	39	12	9	4	21	7	9	

Col. H L. CROKER C.B. (Leicestershire Regt) G.O.C. 81st Bde inspected Battn: on taking over his command.

2nd Battalion The Queen's Own Cameron Highlanders.

Hour, Date, and Place	Summary of Events and Information	Remarks and References to Appendices
CANADA - HUTS 28th March - Sunday 1915	Bn remained in billets in huts. At 10 am G.O.C. 5th Corps inspected the lines. Men were drawn up outside huts & Lt General Sir Herbert Plumer GOC 5th Corps walked round the ranks. At 11 am Battn & A & S.H. paraded for Church Service held by Rev A.S.G. Gilchrist - chaplain to 81st Bde. At 10 pm Officers & N.C.Os who had visited French trenches, returned from YPRES. Digging parties were found as follows C & D 150 men at 6.30 pm A & B. 150 men at 10.30 pm. A draft of 135 men from 3rd Gordons arrived under 2/Lt S.C. Russell 3/Bn (posted to B Coy) 2/Lt A.A. Gemmell reported himself from 10th Liverpool Scottish YPRES. having received a commission & been posted to 2/Bn. (posted to D Coy) Bright Sun - frost & very cold wind	

2nd Battalion The Queen's Own Cameron Highlanders.

Hour, Date, and Place	Summary of Events and Information	Remarks and References to Appendices
CANADA-HUTS 29th March-Monday 1915	Bn. remained in billets in huts. Digging parties found [as follows:- A & B. 150 men at 6.30 - C & D. 150 men at 10.30 - work on G.H.Q. line in rear of CHATEAU - KRUISSTRAATHOEK 2Lts Collier, Cameron & Grant received instruction in bomb throwing] Bright sun - very cold wind - frost.	

2nd Battalion The Queen's Own Cameron Highlanders.

Hour, Date, and Place	Summary of Events and Information	Remarks and References to Appendices
CANAD- HUTS 30th March Tuesday 1915	Bn remained in billets in huts. Orders received that 81st Brigade less 9th Argylls & 9th R. Scots were in reserve to 3rd Divn in trenches. Bn to be ready to turn out at short notice. Capt. G.A. Fowler returned from G/Staff Capt. 71st Bde - & took over command B Coy. 4. Field Kitchens were received in place of 4 limbered wagons returned. Bright sun - cold.	

Capt
adjt

2nd Battalion The Queen's Own Cameron Highlanders.

Hour, Date, and Place	Summary of Events and Information	Remarks and References to Appendices
CANADA - HUTS 31th March-Wed 1915	Bn remained in billets in huts. Continuing with remainder of Bde. to form reserve to 3rd Div in trenches. Work done during day. Coy drill marching S Major parade & Coy inspections. Bright Sun - Cold.	

81st Inf.Bde.
27th Div.

2nd BATTN. THE QUEEN'S OWN CAMERON HIGHLANDERS.

A P R I L

1 9 1 5

2nd Battalion The Queen's Own Cameron Highlanders.

Hour, Date, and Place	Summary of Events and Information	Remarks and References to Appendices
CANADA HUTS (DICKEBUSCH) 1st April Thursday 1915	Bn. remained in billets in huts. At 3 pm. G.O.C. 2nd Army inspected the 81st Brigade at ZEVECOTEN. Bde was drawn up in two lines of close column. Sir Horace Smith-Dorrien walked round the ranks of every company & the machine gun sections. Afterwards the Bde marched home under Sgt Majors - Officers & two N.C.O.s per Coy. remaining. They were addressed by the G.O.C. who commented on past & future work of the Brigade and told them some facts on the general situation. Working parties on G.H.Q. line in rear of Chateau - Kruisstraathoek 300 men in 3 reliefs at 6 - 9.30 & 1 A.M (2nd) from B. C. & D. Coys. 2Lt. A Fraser took over duties of Transport officer from Quartermaster. FINE DAY - warm & bright Sun.	

2nd Battalion The Queen's Own Cameron Highlanders.

Hour, Date, and Place	Summary of Events and Information	Remarks and References to Appendices
CANADA - HUTS 2nd April - Friday (GOOD FRIDAY) 1915	Bn. remained in billets in huts. Orders received that Bn. formed part of a composite Brigade in reserve to 3rd Divn in trenches. Work done during day drill & instruction in sapping - bombing &c. — Dull - colder.	

2nd Battalion The Queen's Own Cameron Highlanders.

Hour, Date, and Place	Summary of Events and Information	Remarks and References to Appendices
CANADA HUTS 3rd April – Saturday 1915	Bn. remained in Billets in huts. Work done during day drill & instruction in Sapping & bombing. Dull – Some rain. Warmer. 		rH	O.R.	h	L.D.	D.	Bag?	Mules	M.G.	4W	2W	Sign?
---	---	---	---	---	---	---	---	---	---	---	---
Effective Strength	26	825	15	39	12	9	3	4	21	7	9
War Establisht	31	976	15	42	12	9		4	21	7	9
To Complete	5	151									
Sick	1	225									
Base & Command		2									
Attached		7									
Strength	27	1052	15	39	12	9	3	4	21	7	9		ˣ Inclusive of M.O. & Chaplain ⁺ 3 mules drawn to complete ° Increase on estb: 1 mun cart 3 hand carts ⁺ Lt Macfarquhar

2nd Battalion The Queen's Own Cameron Highlanders.

Hour, Date, and Place	Summary of Events and Information	Remarks and References to Appendices
CANADA-HUTS to TRENCHES YPRES 4th April - Sunday 1915	At 4.15 pm Bn. marched to YPRES arriving there at 6.40 pm. Halted [there in a ^convent yard] until 8.15 when it moved on via POTIJZE to level crossing 1000 metres N.W. HOOGE. French guides were met there who conducted French parties forward. Trenches occupied 50-60 from S. end of lake (Chateau HERENTHAGE) running NNE to a point 450 yds beyond YPRES - MENIN road. B. Coy on right, C. centre, A. left. D & Bn H.Q. in dugouts N.W. point of HERENTHAGE (INVERNESS) copse about 350 yds from German line. General condition of trenches & dug outs fair, and capable of vast improvement. The line occupied by 27th Divn divided into 2 sections right or south held by 80th & 82nd Bdes, left or north by 57th Bde. Bn held centre portion of left with 9th Argylls on right and 1st Argylls on left. Adv. Bde H.Q. were established in HOOGE. The Regiment French Infantry were relieved in due course & coys settled down. The main road from YPRES being reported dangerous for transport it had to come round to a point 500x S. of WESTHOEK and all stuff carried from there about 1200 yds. Relief complete about 1.30 am. 5th. Casualty wounded No 9890 Pte W. Boyd A Coy. Aid Post established in HOOGE

Fine - cold | |

2nd Battalion The Queen's Own Cameron Highlanders.

Hour, Date, and Place	Summary of Events and Information	Remarks and References to Appendices
TRENCHES (HERENTHAGE) 5th April 1915	Bn. occupied trenches on taken over on 4th. About 11 a.m. enemy shelled portion of wood occupied by Support Coy. Killing one man and wounding three. The 9th Argylls in dugouts across the road also suffered somewhat from enemy's Artillery fire. A very considerable amount of gunfire went on throughout day on both sides - enemy apparently searching for our batteries which were in process of taking over from French. Our guns firing to register ranges. During early part of night a certain amount of material & rations were carried down to trenches from dumping ground. Casualties - Killed No 6337 Pte F. Edwards D. Coy. Shrapnel. Wounded No. 7327 Pte T. Reilly D. Coy Shrapnel " 7939 " J. Michael D. " Shrapnel " S/15579 " W. Craig D. " Shrapnel " S/12858 " S. Hepburn D. " " S/12813 " J. Kirke C " " S/13468 " J. Brodie C " Capt. Bryson M. Officer sent sick. Rain & cold	

2nd Battalion The Queen's Own Cameron Highlanders.

Hour, Date, and Place	Summary of Events and Information	Remarks and References to Appendices
TRENCHES (HERENTHAGE) 6th April - Thursday 1915	Bn. continued to occupy trenches. Fairly quiet day except for continuous artillery fire mostly from our guns registering. Enemy replying occasionally. At about 5 pm enemy opened heavy artillery fire on our left trench occupied by A Coy. This was immediately followed by rapid rifle fire which was replied to - shortly afterwards the incident closed - Beyond some damage to our parapet no great harm was done. A small cemetery was constructed about 100x N. of N.W. corner of INVERNESS COPSE in which men of Bn. were buried. {Pte Cowan LC. Wilson Pte Smith} Casualties Killed No 7356 L.C. J. Wilson A Coy. " S/16370 Pte S. Smith B " (Died of wounds) " 8950 " C. McDonald A " Wounded No. 9025 Cpl. D. Calder C Regimental died of wounds 9/4/15 9050 Pte C. ERNST C " do " S/15501 " A. McGregor A " " S/16334 " A. Robertson A " " S/10739 " T. Curran A " Shell " 8763 " A. McIntosh D " " 9048 " R. Pedan C " A draft of 31 arrived of whom 3 came from base. Rain - Cold	

2nd Battalion The Queen's Own Cameron Highlanders.

Hour, Date, and Place	Summary of Events and Information	Remarks and References to Appendices

TRENCHES (HERENTHAGE) 7th April. Wed. 1915	Bn. occupied trenches. As on last two days considerable artillery fire by day. At night also enemy at very irregular intervals put 3 or 4 shells down YPRES–MENIN road. This appears to be common practice on their part, evidently with a view to denying it to our reliefs & transport.
	
	In evening two men of D. were sniped & hit from enemy's trenches when standing outside support dug-outs. It was noticed that they must have been very visible with sun going down behind them.
	
	Lt Weir R.A.M.C. reported as having taken over duties of Medical Officer vice Capt Bissar.
	
	Casualties. Killed No 8402 Pte W. Gibson D. Coy
	    " 8673 " A. Inglis B "
	    " S/10350 " W. Russell C "
	
	Wounded No 7105 Pte A. Millar C. Coy
	    " S/15887 " W. Nelson C. "
	    " S/17691 " R. McLean C. "
	    " 7755 L.C. R. Houston D. "
	
	Missing No 9740 L/Cpl McKenzie & No 1498 Pte Kennedy A Coy who had been out on patrol the previous night 6th/7th have not returned by dawn & were reported missing (subsequently returned 7th).
	
	Ram Col	

2nd Battalion The Queen's Own Cameron Highlanders.

Gale & Polden, Ltd., Printers, Aldershot. 7,657-u.

Hour, Date, and Place	Summary of Events and Information	Remarks and References to Appendices
TRENCHES (HERENTHAGE) to Close Support in SANCTUARY-WOOD 8th April - Thurs. 1915	Bn. occupied trenches. L/C. McKenzie & Pte Kennedy A. Coy, reported missing on 7th, returned at dusk on 8th. They had crossed German wire & were caught by daylight & remained in a shell hole all day within 7 yds of enemy's parapet. About 2 p.m. Enemy again shelled Hooge & support dug-outs but without doing any damage. By day & night enemy shewed more signs of activity - firing short bursts of rapid from their trenches & sniping continuously. We replied in same way. During the 4 days Sgt Major E Fraser usefully employed his T. Snipers in firing on enemy's fire & communication trenches from selected positions behind our line. Casualties - Wounded At dawn Ptes Gibson, Myles, & Russell were buried in Cemetery. At 9 pm Bn was relieved by 1st R Scots - relief completed 1.30 am - no casualties. Bn moved to Close Support in SANCTUARY-WOOD close to HOOGE & S. of MENIN road - about 1000x further back Dull - some rain - cold	No. 7382 L/Cpl J. Melon B. by shell " 9497 Pte C. McAlister B. " " 3672 " D. McCalman B. Shell " S/15892 " W. Beasant C. " " 8051 " D. Thomson D. "

2nd Battalion The Queen's Own Cameron Highlanders.

Hour, Date, and Place	Summary of Events and Information	Remarks and References to Appendices
SANCTUARY WOOD (Close Support) 9th April - Friday 1915	Bn. occupied dug-outs in N.E. corner of SANCTUARY WOOD just South of MENIN-YPRES road - having taken over from 9th R. Scots the previous evening. Though situated in a hollow about 1200 yds from line on East & 1800 yds from line on South the expended bullets from both directions drop constantly in & around the Wood. An examining guard was found at CASTLE STIRLING (CHATEAU SANS NOM) on main road. After four continuous days in the trenches the men appeared wonderfully fit with none of the exhausted condition they shewed after the first long tour @ St ELOI early in January. The condition of the trenches was of course much better - but moral & experience had - no doubt - a certain amount to do with it. At night carrying parties were found for the Bns in the trenches. The men of draft were posted to Coys Capt I.C. Grant left on leave for England (10 days) Fine - April showers - cold	

2nd Battalion The Queen's Own Cameron Highlanders.

Hour, Date, and Place	Summary of Events and Information	Remarks and References to Appendices
SANCTUARY WOOD. 10th April - Saturday 1915	Bn occupied dug-outs. Work was commenced on constructing washing places for men in small stream running through camp. Also on improving dug-outs and roads through camp. C. Coy by platoons went in to YPRES for change of clothing &c. After dusk C Coy. carried rations & R.E. material from dumping ground to 1/R. Scots H.Q. Two men were hit during this work & one of D. was hit when a platoon of the Coy. were being shewn their position to be taken up, in case of necessity, in subsidiary line which runs from S. of Stirling Castle to Glencorse Wood. Casualties — Wounded No 9617 Pte J. Bryce C. Coy " S/10342 " J. McKendrick C. " " 7114 " D. Lamont D. " Some sun — a little warmer. 15 men more sent to join mining Coy attached 171st Coy R.E.	

	Off	OR	C	LD	D	P	M	MG	4W	2W	B	
Effective Strength	27x	825	15	39	12	9	3	4	21	7	9	x Interpreter MO. & Chaplain
War Establishment	31x	976	15	42	12	9		4	21	7	9	+ 3 mules drawn to complete
To Complete	4	151										
Sick		230										
Base & tomorrow		2										
Attached		7										
Strength	27	1057	15	39	12	9	3	4	21	7	9	

2nd Battalion The Queen's Own Cameron Highlanders.

Hour, Date, and Place	Summary of Events and Information	Remarks and References to Appendices
SANCTUARY WOOD 11th April - Sunday 1915	Bn. remained in Close Support. Work continued on improving condition of dug-outs & surroundings. A good lot of shelling was kept up during day by both sides. No enemy's shells however came near line occupied by Bn. In the morning a French R.E. magazine was seen to explode in neighbourhood of FREZENBERG on YPRES - ZONNEBEKE road; later on orders came that owing to bombs &c being scattered about - the transport would come by MENIN Rd. instead of usual route. Carrying parties were found from D & A Coy for Gloucesters & 1/R. Scots. Draft of 64 arrived 2nd Lt. Macfayden i/c. also 2nd Lt. R.D. Wylie 3rd (posted to D. Coy.) of this draft 40 men were from base. A.B. Coys went in to YPRES for baths. Some Sun - Warmer	

2nd Battalion The Queen's Own Cameron Highlanders.

Hour, Date, and Place	Summary of Events and Information	Remarks and References to Appendices
SANCTUARY WOOD (Close Support) to TRENCHES (INVERNESS COPSE) 12th April - Monday 1915	Bn. remained in close support till evening when it relieved 1/R. Scots who came to close support. In early morning Cd. Adjt. Capt Fowler & B. de May Capt Holland walked over to Glencorse Wood & saw cross erected over grave of Capt Ewan Brodie who was killed in Sept. 14. C. Coy went into YPRES for baths. D Coy found carrying party for R.E. Stores to Gloucester H.Q. 2/Lt D.H. Bell and D. de B. Newcombe joined on first appointment and were posted to C. and A. Coys. A, D, C, B. Coys all in trenches 66 to 56, from left to right each with one platoon in support dug-out @ H.Q. Bn. HQ moved to dug-out 100x S. Menin Road. Work was commenced on communication trenches by supports. During night about 11 pm a ZEPPELIN was reported to have crossed over in W. direction. Casualties Wounded No. 6953 Pte W. Kidd B. Coy. No. 8960 Cpl. A. McLeod " 8324 " J. Ross C. " A Coy Self inflicted. Fine - a little rain	

2nd Battalion The Queen's Own Cameron Highlanders.

Hour, Date, and Place	Summary of Events and Information	Remarks and References to Appendices
TRENCHES (Bois Grenier - Copse) 13th April Tuesday 1915	Re occupied trenches taken over. In morning about 11 o'clock enemy fired several shells into paradox of 57 trench from enfilade position on right - No material damage done -] A quiet day on the whole. Work on communications & improving trenches continued. General condition of trenches not too good, much water collecting. Gum boots which has been called in would prove most useful. × Casualties Killed No. S/12888 Pte R. Laing D. Coy. Wounded No. S/14150 Pte T. Russell A Coy (slightly) " 5442 " T. Colvin A. " " 7557 Cpl R. Allison B. " " 7808 Pte R. McCann B. " shell " 8843 " T. Campbell D. " " S/13402 " T. Percy D. " " 4236 " S. Beach D. " " 5767 " J. Plain D. " " S/15677 " J. Morwood C. " Fire - damer	Pte Laing was buried on 15th in Mervin Cope Cemetery.

2nd Battalion The Queen's Own Cameron Highlanders.

Hour, Date, and Place	Summary of Events and Information	Remarks and References to Appendices
TRENCHES (Inverness Copse) 14th April. Wed. 1915	Bn occupied trenches. In the evening enemy bombed trench 62 in front of an Hermitage. Without much effect – This was obviously in reply to bombing of ours which took place earlier but was not, as it should have been, continued. After dusk work continued on improving trenches & mas. – Material in shape of wood proves scarce & this hinders progress. 2/Lt. Baird-Douglas 3/Bn. joined & was attached to A. Coy. 2/Lt. Giffen admitted to Hospl. Casualties Killed No 7937 L.C. H. Sinclair. B. Coy. Wounded (Died of wounds) No 9172 Pte A. Black A. Coy. Wounded No. 7582 Pte A. Downie A. " " 9/2953 " J. Blair A. " " 8411 " W. Boyd A. " (at duty) " 7431 " A. Martin B. " " 7526 Piper P. Eason B. " " 9014 Pte C. Brown B. " Fine – Warmer	

2nd Battalion The Queen's Own Cameron Highlanders.

HOUR, DATE, AND PLACE	SUMMARY OF EVENTS AND INFORMATION	REMARKS AND REFERENCES TO APPENDICES
TRENCHES (Inverness Copse) 15th April-Thur 1915	Bn. occupied trenches. Enfilade gun again shelled right trenches but did little harm. In evening some bombs were exchanged with Germans - theirs mostly falling short. Enemy put some shells into wood just N. road amongst dug-outs, but without damage. At 5.30 pm orders came that agents reported probable attack on YPRES section of trench line on 15 or 16. A Coy of 1 R. Scots were brought up from Sanctuary Wood & placed under orders of C.O. Other work was carried on as usual, all trenches being warned to be vigilant. Casualties Wounded No. 1/15394 Pte. W. Purves C. Coy @ duty No. 9767. Pte. W. Lennox C. Coy. S.I.	

2nd Battalion The Queen's Own Cameron Highlanders.

Hour, Date, and Place	Summary of Events and Information	Remarks and References to Appendices
TRENCHES (INVERNESS-COPSE) to YPRES. 16th April – Friday 1915	Bn. occupied trenches during day until relieved by 1/R. Scots. At 10.30 am Enfilade gun opened on parados of 57. 58 trenches – application was made to our Arty. who replied & shortly afterwards Enemy's fire ceased. In afternoon one of our Howitzer Battys. shelled a strong position in Enemy's line opposite 68. with some effect. Throughout the tour the Sgt Major actively employed the Snipers. The ground does not lend itself to the work, and most of the sniping has to be done from close to or in the trenches. Relief commenced at 9 pm & was concluded by 11 pm. One man a stretcher bearer was hit at some distance from the trenches. Coys marched by platoons along Menin Rd. to YPRES where the Bn. was billeted in the Hospl Bks – The officers in houses in neighbourhood. Casualties Wounded – Died of Wounds	No/11895 Pte J. McInnes D Coy " 7946 L.C. J. Wilson A.
Buried @ MOOGE 16th " @ YPRES 17th	Wounded No. S/15492 Pte R. Cunningham B. Coy " 5477 " D. McRae B. " " 7324 C/Sgt T. Cameron B. " " 6558 Bdm T. Lennon B. " " 6765 L.C. A. McDonald C. " " S/16414 Pte J. Green C. " " 9737 " T. Clarke C. "	

Fine-Warm
Bar since 9ᵃ R. 5 W. 30

2nd Battalion The Queen's Own Cameron Highlanders.

Hour, Date, and Place	Summary of Events and Information	Remarks and References to Appendices
YPRES. 17th April Saturday 1915	Bn. remained in billets in Hosp¹ Bks. Orders were received to be prepared to turn out @ short notice. About 5 pm heavy artillery fire commenced in S.E. direction which subsequently proved to be part of an organized attack by 5th Div⁰ on a portion of enemy's position on their front — attack was successful after some very heavy & close fighting on the part of the Battalions engaged. Artillery fire was kept up all night and well into morning 18th. News also received that two enemy Aeroplanes had been brought down & captured. Fine — Warm.	

	Off	OR	Ch	LD	D	P	m.	mg	4W	2W	B	
Effective Strength	30	861	15	39	12	9	6	4	21	8	9	*Includes Mob & Chaplain
War Establishm¹	31	976	15	42	12	9		4	21	8	9	*Increase to Cart purchased
To Complete	1	115	✓	✓	✓	✓						
Surplus	✓	✓	✓	✓	✓	✓	3					
Sick	1	176										
Base & Comm		2										
Attached		7										
Strength	31	1089	15	39	12	9	6	4	21	8	9	

2nd Battalion The Queen's Own Cameron Highlanders.

Hour, Date, and Place	Summary of Events and Information	Remarks and References to Appendices
YPRES 18th April Sunday 1915	Bn. remained in billets. Some fairly heavy Artillery fire continued until about 7.30 a.m. and was continued intermittently throughout day. In the evening enemy sent some shells into the town without however doing much damage. At 7.30 pm a digging party of 100 men went out to near WEST HOEK for work on second line - being relieved by 9th Argylls at 11.30 pm. A draft of 121 men arrived of whom 21 were men rejoined from Hosp. C.S.M. McIver came with this draft. Fine - Warm	

2nd Battalion The Queen's Own Cameron Highlanders.

Hour, Date, and Place	Summary of Events and Information	Remarks and References to Appendices
YPRES 19th April - Monday 1915	Bn remained in billets. Came round billets. In the morning enemy shelled E. end of Town - dropping shells in & about billets of Leinster Regt (82nd Bde) causing several casualties. At 7 pm a shell dropped in garden of billet of Bn. H.Q. doing considerable damage to house & slightly wounding two officers. Major L.O. Graeme & 2/Lt J.D. Macleod. The Bn was ordered to hold itself in "constant readiness" during the night - men remaining accoutred ready to turn out at once. Bright Sun - Warmer	At 12.30 pm G.O.C. Divn came round.

2nd Battalion The Queen's Own Cameron Highlanders.

Hour, Date, and Place	Summary of Events and Information	Remarks and References to Appendices
YPRES 20th April Tuesday 1915	Quiet night was passed. About 11 a.m. heavy shelling of the district round headquarters began and it was decided to move the battalion out on the banks of the Yser canal on the N. side of the town. The battalion reached the canal banks about 1.30 p.m.; Heavy shelling of the town continued all day while the battalion remained out of the zone of fire. At 7.30 p.m., when preparing to move on relief to the trenches, a message was received cancelling relief & shortly afterwards the battalion was placed at the disposal of the 5th Division. Lieut. Napier was sent to report at 5th Div. H.Q. for orders. Fine - warm	

2nd Battalion The Queen's Own Cameron Highlanders.

Hour, Date, and Place	Summary of Events and Information	Remarks and References to Appendices
YPRES to trenches S.E. of ZILLEBEKE Tank 21st April 1915. (Wednesday)	At 2.20 a.m. orders were received from the 5th Division placing the battalion at disposal of the 15th Inf. Brigade to whom headquarter Lieut. Tollemache was sent to report. At 3.20 a.m. orders were received for the battalion to move to dug-outs on the west side of ZILLEBEKE tank close to Bde H.Qrs & these were reached at 4.20 a.m. under considerable shell fire, though fortunately without casualties. At 9 a.m. the battalion was ordered to move up in close support of Hill 60 into dug-outs at the Larch Wood & railway cutting 1000 yards south of ZILLEBEKE. The previous night the 1st Devons had relieved the East Surrey's in the trenches & the battalion relieved the Bedfordshire Regt in close support. The C.O. (Lieut. Col. J. Campbell D.S.O.) took over command of the sector, consisting of trenches 38 to 46 & Hill 60, the troops being the 1st Devons, 2nd Cameron Highlanders & the Queen's Westminster Rifles. The remainder of the Brigade sector was occupied by the Cheshires on the left & the Norfolks & Dorsets on the right. Fairly heavy shelling at intervals all the day, Enemy using Gas shells affecting eyes.	
K 1 W 1+12	Casualties. Died of Wounds No.7485 L.C. R. Taylor C. Coy. shell	
	Wounded 2nd Lt L.F. Hussey Macpherson Dy. duty.	No. S/11366 P. W. Kilpatrick C Coy shell
	No. 7216 Pte R. Neil B. Coy shell	S/11859 — W. Shaw C.
	" 9082 " G. Plain B "	8982 — R. Ainslie D
	" 9204 " T. McDonald C. "	S/11142 — A. Conlin D
	" 8783 " J. Blair C. "	S/12837 — J. Forrester D
	" 7564 " J. Donaldson C. "	S/11866 L.C. R. Walker D.
	" 9265 " G. Redpath C. "	

Fric Wann

2nd Battalion The Queen's Own Cameron Highlanders.

Hour, Date, and Place	Summary of Events and Information	Remarks and References to Appendices
Dugs-outs railway cutting S. of ZILLEBEKE. 22nd April 1915. (Thursday) Died of W. 5/5/15 K.L. W.B.	Bn. occupied Dug outs. Buried 25 bodies of various regiments brought down from trenches. Heavy shelling at intervals, a few casualties, fire being caused by our own guns on trench 30 (A coy). Several times during the night bursts of fire broke out of no importance. Effect of gas from shells very noticeable especially in Ry. Cutting & all low lying ground. Caused eyes to water violently & had a sweet pungent taste. Casualties. Died of Wounds 24/4/15 - No. 5760 Cpl. G. McArdle D. Coy Shell Wounded. No. 7737 Pte. C. McFarlane A. Coy shell " 8411 " W. Boyd A " shock. " S/14500 " G. Millar A " " 6655 R. D. Stewart A " Shell " 7803 Pte. T. Murry B " " 7662 " J. McDonald B " " 7714 " R. Fraser B " " 4314 C.S.M. G. McCallum B " " S/13372 Pte. W. Galloway C " " 8158 " T. Campbell C " " 4/6192 " J. Ross C " " 8948 " M. McKenzie D " " 9142 " H. Graham D " Bomb throwers of Northumberland Fusiliers arrived to assist in defence & did good work.	

2nd Battalion The Queen's Own Cameron Highlanders.

HOUR, DATE, AND PLACE	SUMMARY OF EVENTS AND INFORMATION	REMARKS AND REFERENCES TO APPENDICES
23rd April 1915. (Trenches Hill 60) (Friday)	About 1.30 a.m. the Battalion relieved the 1st Devon Regt in trenches 38 to 45. Up to 10 a.m. fairly quiet when enemy commenced firing minenwerfer & howitzer on right & centre of line. Many casualties, much damage where guns turned on. Intermittent throughout day. Captain A. MacDuff & 2nd Lieut. R.R. McIntosh were killed, Captain J.G. Ramsay slightly wounded. Quiet later. The bomb throwers of the Dorsets & the Devons came up for the night also some sappers. Very good work done by companies on repairing the trenches. Water-carts were not allowed to come out & the water supply is somewhat unsatisfactory, having to be carried in supply Amn boxes from ZILLEBEKE TANK. Casualties.— Killed Capt A. MacDuff D.Coy. 2/Lt R.R. McIntosh B.Coy.	
K 2 + 42	15549 Pte R. Lindler A Coy S. S/16347 Pte H. Williamson B. Coy. S	
N 2 + 74	9153 " A. McKenzie A " S. S/15557 " J. McRae B. " S	
	S/14459 " J. Elrick A " S. 7334 " H. Hunter B. " S	
	S/17420 " G. McDade A " S. 9094 A/Cpl G. Mansfield B. " S.	
	S/17711 " D. Holland A " S. 5312 Sgt J. Neald B. " S	
	8059 " M. Crolley A " S. 7700 P. J. Grimmell B. " S.	
	7515 L.C. D. McDonald A " S. 5135 L.C. J. Linkston B. " S.	
	S/12115 P. J. Hay A " S. 7016 P. J. McNab B. " S.	
	7935 " W. Ronaldson A " S. 4905 " A. Rooser B. " S.	
	S/15545 " J. Mearns A " S. 8302 L.C. R. Ney B. " S.	
	S/10289 " F. Freeburn A " B. 9264 " T. Fisher B. "	
	6961 " J. McKenzie A " B. 7605 A/Sgt A. Moure B. "	
	9287 " A. Wilson A " T.M. S/12423 " N. Littlechales B. " S.	
	7606 " G. Sutherland A " T.M. S/16358 " R. Mercer B. " S.	
	S/12009 " J. McAlpine A " T.M. S/15349 " J. Copeland B. " S.	
	S/12542 " B. McKelvie A " T.M. 7403 " W. Hislop B. " S. D of W
	S/16253 L.C. A. Paulinson B. S/16383 " P. Forbes B. " S.	
	7936 Pte A. Baird B. " S. 4597 " A. Symington C. " S.	
	S/16355 " J. Lamont B. " S. 9853 " W. Stirling C. " S.	
	11674 " J. Douglas B. " S.	
	16030 L.C. T. Henderson B. " S.	
	7691 P. J. McAskill B. " S.	
	6140 " G. Allan B. " S.	

2nd Battalion The Queen's Own Cameron Highlanders.

Hour, Date, and Place	Summary of Events and Information	Remarks and References to Appendices
HILL 60. Cont^d 23rd April. Friday 1915 D of W. 26th × D. of W. 23rd D of W. 25th D of W. 3/5/15.	Casualties Continued - Wounded Capt. J.G. Ramsay A Coy. Shell - Capt. I.C. Grant. C. Coy. Shell. 7142 P. J. McShane A Coy. S. S/14411 P. H. McQueen B. Coy. Shock 7906 " W. Paterson A " S. 9314 " J. Fraser B. " S/12952 " D. Carmichael A " S. 9176 " J. Stewart B. " Shock 5645 " G. Gardner A " S. S/14412 " J. Duff B. " S. 8672 L.C. R. Athya A " S. S/15570 " N. McPherson B. " shock S/10757 P.P. McCall A " S. S/11697 " O. Jamieson B. " S. 7924 " W. Poulton A " S. S/15571 " W. Hutcheson B. " Shock 7536 " H. Ferguson A " S. 7424 " A. Ralph B. " S. S/9421 " J. Flint A " S. S/11854 " A. Walker B. " 6579 " T. Rutherford A " S. 9212 " J. McDonald B. " S/15508 " A. McGregor A " B. 7022 L.C. A. Aitken C. " S. 6901 " T. Finnie A " S. 7035 P. J. Campbell C. " Shock 6791 " W. Bear A " S. 9168 L.C. A. Dudgeon C. " S. 9721 " M. Kirkaldy A " S. 9006 P. J. Flynn C. " S. S/14451 " A. Kerr A " Shock 6153 " J. Waterson C. " Shock 9758 " A. Clark A " S/15004 " P. Kerr C. " Shock 5876 " W. Gall A " Shock S/5011 Sgt. D. Morrison C. " S. S/10575 " L. Nicolson A " S/16421 P. W. Fotheringham C. " 8162 " F. McKenzie A " S/15572 " J. O'Rorke C. " Shock 9140 " G. Main A " S. 15383 " P. White C. " Shock S/14956 " J. Hollinger A " Shock S/15897 Cpl. C. Anderson C. " Shock 7087 L.C. W. Wallace A " " S/16205 P. T. Walker C. " S. S/16245 P. J. McGregor A " S. S/16669 " A. Bowman C. " Shock 5659 " J. Carrigan A " Shock 7630 " A. McIntyre A " S. 7903 " H. Brown A " S. S/14075 " D. Dunlop A " Shock 9235 " J. Teasdale A " S. 7712 " T. Galbraith A " S. 7353 " W. Budge A " S. 9056 " F. Stewart A " S. 7953 " J. Robertson A " S. 9242 " J. Aikman A " Shock S/11703 " J. Higgins A " S. S/11153 L.C. J. Anderson A " Shock S/17580 P. J. Rowe B. " S/14414 " G. McGregor B. " S. S/11935 " D. Inglis B. " S. 8146 " T. Taylor B. " S. S/11858 " H. Matthews B. " S. S/16333 " P. Forbes B. " S. S/15560 " J. Christie B. " S. S/15561 " J. Christie B. " S. 8095 " J. Innes B. " S. 7940 " A. Fraser B. " S. 3/696 " J. Boyle B. " Shock 7755 " J. Brown B. " S. 7140 " J. Nelson B. " S. 6665 L/Sgt. A. Douglas B. " S. duty 6349 P. A. McIntosh B. " S. 7721 " W. Hussan B. " S.	

2nd Battalion The Queen's Own Cameron Highlanders.

Hour, Date, and Place	Summary of Events and Information	Remarks and References to Appendices
24th April 1915. (Trenches) ZILLEBEKE (Saturday) K 3 W 25	Bn. occupied trenches. A quiet night & a much quieter day than yesterday. On each occasion on which the enemy's minenwerfer or howitzers started on our trenches our guns were turned on & silenced them. Very good work was done by the battalion in repairing & strengthening the trench line. Casualties Killed No. 8333 L.C. W. McDiarmid A S. " 7242 P. J. Syme C S. " S/15341 " R. McKendrick D. Wounded No. 9058 Pte. S. Blakely A Coy G. " S/13021 " J. Addison A " Shock " S/16664 " W. Devries A " S. " S/15010 " F. Connelly A " Shock " 7517 " A. Venners A " S. " 7440 L.C. J. Thomson B " S. " S/5862 P. P. McCann B " " S/15065 " D. Binet B " S. " 11946 LC J. Lyall B " Shock " 8018 P. D. McGlone B " " " S/11580 " A. Hay B " " 8974 " G. Robertson B " S. " 7172 A/Cpl W. Patterson B " Shock " 7840 L.C. J. McGeachy C " " 9422 " J. McGillan C " " 9157 P. G. Stewart C " S. " S/14425 " W. Young C " S. " S/15464 " J. Gray C " S. " 3/5405 " A. McMillan C " S. " S/15469 " A. Ness C " S. " 3/5445 " J. Cameron C " S. " 7107 " T. Reid C " " 8210 " J. McIntyre C " Shock " 9239 " W. McIntosh D " S. " S/14438 L.C. W. Dimoon D " S. Effective Strength O/R 31 969 Sick 31 976 To Complete 1 Sick + Details 170 Strength 31 1139	

2nd Battalion The Queen's Own Cameron Highlanders.

Hour, Date, and Place	Summary of Events and Information	Remarks and References to Appendices

25th April 1915
ZILLEBEKE
(Sunday)
 	
D of W 27/4
	By 10 a.m. all companies were relieved from the trenches by the 1st Devons & returned to close support into dug-outs some 300 or 400 yards in rear of the front line. There was a great deal of heavy gun & musketry firing during the day to the north & East of YPRES. 2nd Lieut. D.H. Bell was ~~lightly~~ wounded by shrapnel. The rations, water & R.E. Stores for ourselves & the Devons were carried up by the battalion from Brigade H.Q. to these dug-outs & to the trenches. A quiet day on our portion of the line.
	Casualties Killed No. 4454 L/Cpl J. McEwan C. Coy. S.
	2 " S/15453 P. T. Scott D. "
	Wounded 2/Lt. D.H. Bell C. Coy. S.
	1 + 11 7421 Pte A. Ramage A. "
	  1787 " W. Knowles A. " S. duty
	  9309 " J. Bothwell B. " Shock
	  5357 a/Sgt. J. Taylor B. " S.
	  9174 Pte P. H. Hosey C. " S.
	  9113 " A. Johnstone C. " S.
	  9105 " F. Reid C. " S.1
	  3/6244 " J. Fraser C. " S.
	  3/18344 " H. Bell C. " S.
	  9295 " J. McArthur C. " S.
	  S/15955 " D. Munro D. " S.	

2nd Battalion The Queen's Own Cameron Highlanders.

Hour, Date, and Place	Summary of Events and Information	Remarks and References to Appendices
26th April 1915. ZILLEBEKE (Monday)	Bn. occupied dug-outs in Support. A good deal of intermittent artillery fire was in progress during the morning. At 2 p.m. to the N.E. of YPRES a combined attack of the French & British commenced. About this hour there was a considerable burst of the enemy's artillery fire on the front trenches held by the Devons & over our dug-outs in support. Captain & Adjutant A.D. Macpherson was slightly wounded in the neck & hand by a splinter from a shell. The sound of very heavy fighting to the N.E. continued until nightfall. Lieut. G. Murray rejoined for duty and Lieut. G. Gordon was placed on the sick list. Casualties Killed 8551 A/Cpl. R. Allison B. Coy. Wounded Capt. Adjt. A.D. Macpherson H.Q. S. 8653 Sgt. D. Monro A Coy S. duty. 7340 Pte. A. Campbell A " S. 9268 " G. Carr B " S. S/6459 " P. Anderson B " Shock 9756 Cpl. C. Ryan C " S.I duty. 4346 R.Sgt.Maj E. Fraser C " S. duty. 16960 Pte. W. Sellars C " S. 13113 " H. Clark D " S.	K 1 W 1+8

2nd Battalion The Queen's Own Cameron Highlanders.

Hour, Date, and Place	Summary of Events and Information	Remarks and References to Appendices
27th April 1915 ZILLEBEKE (Trenches) Tuesday.	About 2 a.m. the battalion relieved the Devons in the front trenches. The night was quiet & little firing went on in our immediate front. 2nd Lieut. D. De B. Newcome temporally took over the duties of acting Adjutant to the battalion. Slight bombing of the trenches went on. [Lieut. C.W. Mills received a slight graze on head from bullet] A draft of forty eight men joined the battalion & were posted to companies in the trenches.	
K 1 W 1+2	Casualties Killed No 17319 Pte T. Wagstaff B. Coy. Wounded 2Lt. C. M. Mills C Coy — duty. 8429 P. F Mitchell B " B. 5647 " A Boyd A " S	

2nd Battalion The Queen's Own Cameron Highlanders.

Hour, Date, and Place	Summary of Events and Information	Remarks and References to Appendices
28th April 1915 ZILLEBEKE (Trenches) Wednesday.	Bn. occupied fire trenches. From 2 a.m. until daybreak a very heavy artillery combat continued at some miles distance to the N.E. otherwise the enemy was inactive opposite our trenches. From about 10.30 a.m. to 12 noon several bombs from Minenwerfer were fired at the front trenches particularly at Hill 60. About 12 noon the enemy succeeded in landing one of these bombs right into the trench on the hill causing the greatest damage & loss. Captain A. A. Fowler & 2nd Lieut. D. Grant as well as eight men were killed by the explosion and seven others were wounded or severely damaged by the concussion. Considerable difficulty experienced in effecting repairs to the parapet of this trench as the earth of the hill is loose & crumbly & continually keeps slipping back into the crater behind. No further incident occurred during the day.	

K 2+7
W 4
M 1
	Casualties Killed Capt. A. A. Fowler B. Coy. B.
	                 2 Lt. D. Grant B. " B.
	            S/12401 Pte J. Baird B. " B.
	            8358 " T. Ramsay B. " B.
	            S/16166 " A. Davidson B. " B.
	            7423 L.C. D. Dow B. " B.
	            9100 P. G. Kincaid B. " B.
	            S/16249 " A. Russell B. " B.
	            S/16717 " J. Brown B. "
	Wounded 15375 Pte A. Turner B. Coy Shock
	            15374 " T. Gibson B. "
	            8554 " T. Oss B. " S1
	            7872 " P. McCune B. "
	Missing S/15498 R. Cunningham B.	

2nd Battalion The Queen's Own Cameron Highlanders.

Hour, Date, and Place	Summary of Events and Information	Remarks and References to Appendices
29th April 1915. (Thursday) ZILLEBEKE Trenches to Support	About 1.30 a.m. the enemy exploded a mine at Hill 60, but as the charge was fired somewhere just to the left front of the hill no damage was done. Between 2 a.m. & 3 a.m. the battalion was relieved by the 1st Devons & returned into the support dug-outs at Larch Wood. During the whole of the night the enemy kept sending, every five minutes, a high velocity small shrapnel shell over these dug-outs. This shelling ceased about daybreak. Comparative quiet during the day. Orders were received for the Battalion to rejoin the 81st Bde & that for the present they would act as a Divisional reserve battalion. About 11 p.m. the 1st Dorsets relieved us & the battalion moved off by platoons to the wood in the grounds of the Chateau at Potigze.	
D.o.W. 6/5/15	Casualties Wounded S/14500 P. G. Millar A Coy. S.	
	8928 L/C. J. Bannerman A " S. duty	
	S/15481 P. D. McDonald B " S.	
	S/15596 " J. Wilson B " S.	
	4584 L/C. G. Cox B " S.	
	8872 P. D. Blair B " S.	
D.o.W. 4/5/15	8466 P. A. McArthur B " S.	
	Cas. while with 5th Div. K. 4+58. W. 6+156. M.1.	

2nd Battalion The Queen's Own Cameron Highlanders.

Hour, Date, and Place	Summary of Events and Information	Remarks and References to Appendices
30th April 1915 (Friday) POTIJZE K 3 W 12 D of W - 1/5/15	Owing largely to the neighbourhood of our batteries, a heavy shelling of this wood goes on day & night from three sides. The cover available for the men is exceedingly poor & with the tools available, only the entrenching ones carried by the men, it was difficult to improve it very largely. At 8 p.m. the battalion moved out as a working party to dig a line of trenches at ARRET & returned about 2 a.m. the following morning. Captain D. Cameron & Lieut. J. R. H. Anderson joined to-day for duty. Casualties Killed 8869 P. J. Sandilands B. Coy. S. 5390 " J. Aberdeen B. " S. 5/16087 " S. Kerr D. " S. Wounded 7659 L.C. W. Cameron A. Coy. S. 5/11121 P. A. Nelson B. " S. 5/14483 " T. Hicks B. " S. 5/15596 " J. Wilson B. " S. 5/9777 " N. Hanson B. " S. 5/15280 " A. Graham C. " S. 7546 " A. Lawson C. " S. 6656 " H. Cumberford C. " S. duty 8926 " R. Henderson C. " S. 5/16414 " J. Green C. " S. duty 5/16187 " W. Roy C. " S. 5/13125 " W. Barnard D. " S.	

81st Inf.Bde.
27th Div.

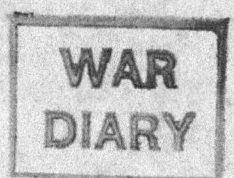

2nd BATTN. THE QUEEN'S OWN CAMERON HIGHLANDERS.

M A Y

1 9 1 5

2nd Battalion The Queen's Own Cameron Highlanders.

Hour, Date, and Place	Summary of Events and Information	Remarks and References to Appendices
1st May 1915 (Saturday) POTIJZE.	The enemy's shelling ceased during the morning. A heavy bombardment however broke out again in the course of the afternoon. At 7 p.m. the battalion again moved out to carry on the improvement of the trench lines where they were digging last night, with orders that on completion of the task they were to move to a fresh bivouac in ZOUAVE wood immediately S.W. of HOOGE. Casualties Killed 7741. Pte R Heatley B Coy S	
D of W. 2/5/15	Wounded 7126 LC J Thomson D Coy S S/13010 P. W Stone A . S S/13153 " R Liston A . S 9825 " J Lockhart B . S 3/5833 " R Marr C . S 6686 " N Cumberford C . S S/10446 " C Stewart C . S 8552 " J Fee C . S S/16677 " J McCaw C . S S/16229 LC W Sinclair C . S 6258 " R Sinclair C . S 9887 " W Mackie D . S	

Effective Strength Off 25 O.R. 787
Estab. 31 976
To Complete   189
Sick 1 322
Base   2
Strength 26 1111

2nd Battalion The Queen's Own Cameron Highlanders.

Hour, Date, and Place	Summary of Events and Information	Remarks and References to Appendices
2nd May 1915. (Sunday) ZOUAVE WOOD.	About 2 a.m. the last company had reached their bivouac in this wood. At 10 a.m. work was commenced on the construction of dug-outs all round this wood, the intention being to make it fit for close occupation by the battalion in support of the trench lines. At 5 p.m., owing to an attack by the enemy on some trenches north of POTIJZE, an order was received for the 2nd Camerons & 9th Royal Scots to move at once under Lieut. Col. J. Campbell to the wood of the Chateau at that place. This move was carried out quickly under a very heavy shell fire but without a casualty. The German attack having being driven back the services of the battalion were not however called upon & by 10 p.m. all companies were back in ZOUAVE WOOD. 2nd Lieut. Baird-Douglas was placed on the sick list. Casualties. Wounded 4. 7976 L.C. J. Blythe B. Coy. 3/5755 P. M. Morrison B " 9254 " P. Carlin C " J. 8204 " J. Quigley D " S.	

2nd Battalion The Queen's Own Cameron Highlanders.

Hour, Date, and Place	Summary of Events and Information	Remarks and References to Appendices
3rd May 1915 (Monday) ZOUAVE WOOD.	At 1 a.m. A. B & D companies found working parties for making entrenchments, these companies got back to bivouac at daybreak. At 10 a.m. & throughout the rest of the day the whole battalion was working making & strengthening the trench line across the MENIN road & running along the east side of SANCTUARY wood. About 4.30 p.m. the 2nd Cameron Highdrs & 9th Royal Scots again received orders to move out in a northerly direction & report to the 85th I.Bde at VELORENHOCK for orders as it was anticipated that reinforcements might be required on that flank of the line. Just before arrival at that place the heavy shell fire was opened on the battalion as it was on the move, the best available cover was at once occupied but several casualties occurred. Lieut. L.F. Hussey-Macpherson and Lieut. A.A. Gemmell were wounded during this shelling. The services of the battalion during the evening were lent in turn to the 85th, 11th & 83rd Inf. Brigades without however eventually being required by any one of them. About 11 p.m. orders were received for the battalion to return to its own bivouac & back to the 81st Inf. Brigade. Casualties Killed 1 6347 Pte R. Dewar A Coy S. Wounded 2+8 Lt L.F. Hussey-Macpherson D Coy S. 9/6086 Pte J. M°Luckie A Coy S. " Lt A.A. Gemmell D " S. 6087 Sgt T. Cunningham D " S. 8853 Sgt D. Morris A " S. 8853 L/Sgt A. Stewart A " S. 16302 Pte J. M°Guire A " S. 8813 " J. Clark A " S. 8/15201 " A. Murray A " S. 6547 " T. Renfrew A " S.	

Philipt
Adjt

2nd Battalion The Queen's Own Cameron Highlanders.

Hour, Date, and Place	Summary of Events and Information	Remarks and References to Appendices
4th May 1915. (Tuesday) ZOUAVE WOOD.	The battalion returned to its bivouac about 1.30 a.m. Considerable & intermittent shelling of the wood went on during the day, the companies were however scattered about over a large area & there were not many casualties. The trench line formerly occupied by the 27th & 28th Divisions had during the previous night been considerably withdrawn & in consequence shortened, this naturally tended to bring fresh areas under the direct fire & view of the enemy. At 8 p.m. the battalion took over & occupied the allotted portion of the new trench line relieving the 1st Royal Scots. The line at this part crossed the YPRES-MENIN road at a point immediately east of HOOGE. Battalion headquarters being at the west end of HOOGE in some spacious old French dug-outs S of Road. The new trenches required a great deal of work on them as there had been insufficient time to prepare them beforehand & hard work was done at them during the night. Casualties Wounded 16 5745 Pte G. Wells A Coy S. 4059 CSM N. McIver B Coy 7945 " R. Duff A " S. 7560 L/Cpl A. Hay. D " S. 8750 " W. Alexander A " 7716 P. A McKenzie D " S. 3/2919 Sgt. M. McIver A "accidental" 9/5907 P. J. Shelton D " S. 8608 L.C. J. Duncan A . S. 3/6012 " J. McKinnon D " S. 9206 P. J. Mowbray A " S. 16420 " R. Robertson D " S. D of W 5th 8378 L/Cpl W. Goodall B. S. 15919 " R. Reid D " S. 7464 P. W. Wilkinson C " S 9/11553 " D. McKendry D " S.	

2nd Battalion The Queen's Own Cameron Highlanders.

Hour, Date, and Place	Summary of Events and Information	Remarks and References to Appendices
5th May 1915. (Wednesday) HOOGE Trenches.	Consistent shelling of the trench line and of the supports by the enemy continued throughout the day. At present in this area the Germans have a distinct superiority in the number & size of their artillery. [2nd Lieut. N.D. MacFadyen was killed by a shell bursting in the trench.] Trenches still very poor and in the low parts where the ground is swampy they are exceedingly wet & difficult to work on. Weather continues fine and is getting much warmer. 2nd Lieut. D. de B. Newcomb, acting Adjutant, slightly wounded in the leg by a shrapnel splinter and had to be sent to hospital. 2nd Lieut. A.L. Collier took over the duties of Adjutant temporally. A quiet night both sides working hard at their defences. Casualties Killed 1 & 3 2/Lt. N.D. MacFadyen A. Coy. S. 5202 Sgt L. Spencer A " S. S/16719 L.C. G. Finlayson A " S. 8917 P. M. McKay A " S. Wounded 12 S/17304 Pte R. Fleming A. Coy. S. 8827 S.C.A Cosgrove C " S. S/14424 P. J. Headspeath C " S. 7911 " H. Craig C " S. S/14460 " W. Henderson C " S. S/16546 " J. McNeil C " S. 1/11709 " W. Moodie D " S. 9/13972 " R. Bart D " S. S/17456 " W. Fraser B " S. 8991 " A. McRae B " S. S/10755 " J. Stewart B " S. S/10664 " J. Bowman B " S.	

2nd Battalion The Queen's Own Cameron Highlanders.

Hour, Date, and Place	Summary of Events and Information	Remarks and References to Appendices

6th May 1915 (Thursday) HOOGE Trenches.	Bn occupied Trenches. A comparatively quiet day was spent & the enemy did not shell the trenches nearly so much as yesterday. The enemy's present line averages some four hundred yards from ours. Weather sultry & warm.
	
	Casualties Wounded 8710 Pte A. Smith A Coy
	     1+3 7893 " W. Oliphant A " S.
	         S/16670 " G. McDonald B "
	Adjt 2Lt D de B. Newcombe H.Q. S.	

2nd Battalion The Queen's Own Cameron Highlanders.

Hour, Date, and Place	Summary of Events and Information	Remarks and References to Appendices
7th May 1915. (Friday) HOOGE Trenches.	Bn. occupied Trenches. Quiet night. At about 2.30 a.m. there was some restlessness owing largely to firing which was going on at some distance on our right & left, about 3 a.m. the enemy shelled the woods in rear of the trenches where our supports are located. There was less shelling today than usual and enemy quiet. Received orders that Brigade is to give up 100ᵡ of trenches on right to 82nd Bde. and to take over 300ᵡ on left from 80th Bde. to take effect tomorrow night. Battns. to be relieved night 9/10th. Major L.O. Graeme proceeded this evening to take over command of 1st Battalion. Fine and muggy day. Casualties Wounded 2 8692 L/Cpl. J. Campbell. A Coy. 7949 P. R. Robertson D. " S.	

2nd Battalion The Queen's Own Cameron Highlanders.

8th

39

Hour, Date, and Place	Summary of Events and Information	Remarks and References to Appendices
8th May 1915. (Saturday) HOOGE Trenches. Wounded 39 7157 L.C. F. Moir C.Coy 5/16199 P.D. Dinnie B-S 3/1027 " Comer D-S 8132 " B. McQuillan A-S 9090 " G. Galloway B-S 5/16348 " N. Kinstie B-S 5511 " R. Gillies B-S 7350 " R. Anderson B-S 8550 " A. McDonald B-S 5/16656 " W. Connelly B-S 5/16422 " J. Neill B-S 11076 " J. Donaldson B-S 3/16276 " N. Fowler B-S 5041 " J. McCulloch B-S 5/11095 " G. Stewart B-S 8040 L.C.H. Culbertson C-S duty 8557 P. M. Hummel C-S duty 9/5707 " J. Young C-S 8131 " A. Clark C-S 8582 " A. Reid C 7409 Pte J. Gilson C-S 8156 L.C. S. Hatton C-S 3/5637 P.D. Campbell C 717 " S. Davies D-S 5/12660 " Kennie D-S 7707 " J. Munson D-S 7059 L.C. J. Crichton D-S 7120 SjtJ. Hogg D-S 5/16476 P.A. McGuinness D-S 7501 " A. Mitchell D-S 8614 " H. Wilson D-S 9073 " J. Houston D-S 5/13110 " J. Low D-S 9575 " C. Flynn D-S 5/16886 " C. Hunter D-S 5/13094 " A. Connell D-S 9008 " A. Briggs D-S 11882 " W. Greenshields D-S 5/12428 " R. Wemyss D-S	Quiet night. About 7 a.m. heavy bombardment by enemy began directed on area N. of MENIN road and HOOGE became intense 8.45 to 9 a.m. then slackened increasing again at 9.20. About 10 a.m. the Reserve (C) company was ordered to reinforce 4th K.R.R. who had suffered considerably from enfilade arty. fire. The company accordingly reinforced trenches from East entrance to HOOGE CHATEAU Square J.13.a.5.9. to the left of our batton. D Coy. at hedge 30 yds. N. of MENIN road. J.13.a.5.3. About 10.30 a.m. 9.a.+5. Hfrs came up and occupied 2nd line trenches in support. At 11 a.m. there was a distinct lull. About 1 p.m. Leinster Regt. came into support in 2nd line trenches SANCTUARY WOOD. 1.15 to 1.45 SANCTUARY WOOD and HOOGE bombarded with heavy shells. During this period A and B Coys holding right and centre and D left of our line had not been attacked and had not suffered many casualties. By 1 p.m. the situation south of BELLEWAARDE POND was established and quiet. enemy reported entrenching about CLAPHAM JN. and to the north. Towards evening the situation became quieter. It was understood that the right 28th Div. had given way and about 12 mn 1st R. Scots arrived from 'rest' and the possibility of a withdrawal to the 2nd line and to S.W. corner of LAKE BELLEWAARDE was indicated to Cos. A.B.C Coys were therefore employed in post (support platoons) in preparing this line. Fine bright day. Casualties Killed 8	

	Offrs.	O.R.
Effective Strength	20	752
Casualties	31	976
To Complete	11	224
Sick	2	376
Bail		2
Strength	24	1130

5/12024	Pte	J. Watson	A Coy	S.
8157	L.S.	M. McDonald	B "	S.
5/10439	P.	M. Boyle	C "	
5/10496	"	J. Burns	C "	
5/15547	"	J. Boyd	C "	
8697	LC	O. Stevenson	C "	S.
5/11079	"	J. Purvers	D "	S.
5/15500	"	J. Watson	D "	S.

2nd Battalion The Queen's Own Cameron Highlanders.

Hour, Date, and Place	Summary of Events and Information	Remarks and References to Appendices
9th May 1915 (Sunday) HOOGE Trenches.	About 4 a.m. information was received that 80th Brigade holding trenches N.E. of LAKE BELLEWAARDE had been ordered back to a line from N.W. corner connecting with 28th Divn. on the railway - the line south from the S.E. arm of the lake to be held as before. A heavy attack again developed on the left but line was maintained. During the night Cavalry line S of Lake BELLEWARDE was reconnoitred & strengthened with a view to possible withdrawal in the morning. Supporting Posts in direction of YPRES also prepared. Severe shelling about 6·0 p.m. 2nd Lt L.R.M. Napier wounded (severe) Casualties Killed 2 9665 C/Sgt D. McCaig B Coy. S. 7796 Pte D. McAulay C. " Wounded 1+22 S/10353 Pte D. Laird A Coy S 7450 " J. Dunlop A " Shock S/12886 " T. Campbell A " S 7263 L.C. J. Davis B " S S/15891 Pte G. Cairns B " S 7945 " G. McCaig B " S 7476 " H. Reid B " S S/13343 " W. Sommerville B " S S/16676 " J. McMurdo B " S 7232 L.C. W. Anderson B " S S/16659 Pte T. Colvine B " G. 9269 " J. Taylor B " S S/17704 " J. Green B " G 9061 A/Cpl A. Reid B " G S/14918 Pte A. Cummings B " S S/12780 " A. Mitchell B " S 9315 " N. Crisp C " S 7472 " A. Munro C " S 6124 C.S.M. G. Martin D " S/13787 Pte D. Hardie D " S 9559 " A. Graham D " S. 9836 " R. McKenzie B " S.I	D. of W. 13th D. of W. 14th D. of W. 13th

2nd Battalion The Queen's Own Cameron Highlanders.

Hour, Date, and Place	Summary of Events and Information	Remarks and References to Appendices
10" May 1915 Hooge (Trenches) Monday.	Night passed quietly time employed strengthening position. Companies in same position as before A. B. D less 1 Platoon S of MENIN ROAD 1 Platoon "D" & no 9 Platoon C. N of MENIN Rd. in touch with 4th K.R.R. Heavy bombardment opened about 7.0 am. becoming intense about 10 am. directed principally at trenches N of MENIN Road & Chateau Woods. About 10 am. a number of K.R.R. & "C" Company came back on support trenches but were checked & moved forward & re occupied front line again which meanwhile was being enfiladed from left. Bombardment about 4 pm became intense & enemy attacked under cover of gas & shell fire. All troops N of MENIN Rd. driven back on support (Cavalry) line. D Company inspite of their left being exposed hung on very gallantly and defeated all efforts of the Germans to force them from their trench. In spite of heavy losses line maintained till evening. "D" Coy supported by Company 1/9 Argyll & S.H. who lost very heavily in comm't trench enfiladed by M.G. About 4 pm Col Campbell D.S.O. took over a sector of the line & directed Capt D Cameron to take cmd of the Bn. temporarily. Casualties incurred during the day. Killed. 2Lt Caddenhead. Wounded Lt Russell, 2nd Lt R Cameron about 150 Rank & File K. W & M. At 11.0 pm. a draft of 130 including details from base arrived under Captain A.C. Sampson & following Officers :— Capt. P.L. McCall, Lt. Henderson, Lt. A. Leah, 2 Lt G.S. McKay	

Casualty List 10th May 1915

K 1 + 22
3 + 78
M 19

Date	No.	Rank	Name	Killed	Wd.	Coy.	Date	No.	Rank	Name	Killed	Wd.	Coy.
10th May	9158	Pte	J Donnachie	K		A	10th May	S/14093	Pte	B. Preston		W	B.
	4246	"	A Broadfoot	K		A		8451	"	R. McGregor		W	B.
	4655	"	J. Smith	K		D		4566	"	B. Stoole		W	B.
	8733	L/Cpl	P. Healey	K		C.		S/12864	"	J. Brown		W	B.
	8459	a/Cpl	K. McHattie	K		C.		8461	"	A. McMillan		W	C.
	S/15589	Pte	J Grant	K		C.		S/15205	"	H. Dearden		W	C.
	8932	"	J. McAulay	K		B.		8832	"	K. Ferguson		W	C.
	9344	"	A Hendry	D of W		B		S/14638	"	D Cameron		W	C.
	S/5919	"	A Craig	K		B		S/16126	"	J. Ewing		W	C.
	8918	Cpl	A Kennedy	K		D		9094	a/Cpl	W. Gibson		W	C.
	S/12966	Pte	J Clark	K		D		S/5500	Pte	A. McIntosh		W	C.
	S/16384	"	A Lawrie	K		D		8963	a/Cpl	W. Cameron		W	C.
	4985	L/Cpl	A French	K		D		4905	Pte	J Maurice		W	C.
	S/12950	Pte	W. Holmes	K		D		4219	"	M Love		W	A.
	S/16366	"	J. Crichton	K		D		4144	"	R. Wilson		W	C.
	11310	"	J. Donald	K		D		S/14440	"	J. Semple		W	C.
	8686	"	D. Page	K		D		S/14324	"	H. Downie		W	C.
	8324	"	P. Falconer	K		D		8040	L/Cpl	A Cuthbertson		W	C.
	8640	"	J. Brown	K		C.		S/15641	Pte	J O'Neill		W	C.
	S/11101	"	C. Cochrane	D of W		C.		4955	Sgt.	A Colvine		W	C.
	S/6022	"	G. Haywood	K		B		9041	L/Cpl	D Doig		W	C.
		Lt.	G. Cadenhead	K		D		S/14442	Pte.	J. Scott		W	C.
	8349	Pte	W. McGhee		W	D.		8464	"	D. McIntyre		W	C.
	S/13004	L/Cpl	J. Simpson		W	A.		4865	L/Cpl	Y. Dahill		W	D.
	8482	"	W. McLaney		W	C.			2/Lt	H. Leah		W	A
	8139	Pte	S. McAleer	D of W	11/5/15	G.			Lt.	K. Cameron	Gas		Y.
	8865	a/Cpl	R. Hocking		W	D		S/15849	Pte.	J. Reid		W	B.
	8614	Pte	A. Wilson		W	D		S/15840	"	W. Harrold		W	B.
	8282	"	Y. Elder		W	A		S/16515	"	W. Robertson		W	B.
	8480	L/Cpl	A. Henderson		W	A		6434	a/Cpl	A. Jarvie		W	D.
	8928	"	J. Bannerman		W	A		9144	Pte.	H. Skeet		W	D.
	4686	"	J. Cox		W	A		4486	"	A McKenzie		W	D.
	S/15683	Pte.	T. Stoddart		W	A		4935	"	H. Reid		W	D.
	S/13638	"	S. McMillan		W	A		S/15361	"	A. Dewar		W	D.
	S/12419	"	A. Smith		W	A		9350	"	A. Campbell		W	D.
	S/14614	"	A. Moore		W	A		11190	"	A. Cameron		W	D.
	5143	Sgt	J. Arthur		W	B.		S/12951	"	A. McLennan	D of W	14/5/15	D.
	8595	"	J. Simpson		W	B.		S/13103	"	A. Johnstone		W	D.
	8996	Cpl	R. Scott		W	B.		8731	"	D. Millar		W	D.
		Lt.	L.R.M. Napier		W	B							
	9041	a/Cpl	A. Walker		W	B.							
	8250	L/Cpl	Y. McGill		W	B							

Casualty List (Contd) 10th May 1915

Date	No	Rank	Name	Killed	Wd.	Coy	Date	No	Rank	Name	Killed	Wd.	Coy
10th May	S/5845	Pte	A. McIntyre	Gas		D	10th May	7775	Pte	J. Cranston	missing		D
	7852	"	A. Irving		W	D		8126	"	A. McLeich	missing		D
	7923	Cpl	R. Stewart		W	D							
	S/15919	Pte	A. Nash		W	D							
	S/15404	"	J. Lindsay		W	C							
	S/14016	"	A. Ross		W	C							
	6474	"	D. McIntyre		W	B							
	13314	"	J. Bell		W	D							
	7423	"	J. Carswell		W	D							
	8398	"	J. Douggans		W	D							
	7584	"	W. Morrison		W	D							
	S/11846	"	G. Docherty		W	D							
	S/12941	Cpl	C. McLure		W	D							
	S/12944	Pte	A. Davidson		W	D							
	S/12424	"	H. Whitaker		W	D							
	S/10842	"	G. Percy		W	D							
	S/12948	"	A. Anderson		W	D							
	S/15892	"	H. McMillan		W	D							
	S/6051	"	R. Manners		W	D							
	8050	"	D. Thomson		W	D							
	9410	"	L. Holmes		W	D							
	7301	"	J. Forsyth		W	D							
	8364	"	P. Mitchell		W	D							
	8439	"	R. Barr		W	D							
	6699	Sgt	M. McDonald	missing		C							
	7846	"	C. Cameron	missing		C							
	8210	Cpl	L. McKellor	missing		C							
	9218	Pte	J. McIntyre	missing		C							
	S/12947	"	W. Mathie	missing		C							
	S/13113	"	W. McArthur	missing		C							
	6459	"	J. Brown	missing		C							
	S/15842	"	J. McWhinnie	missing		C							
	S/16134	"	A. Downie	missing		C							
	8922	"	A. Baird	missing		C							
	8318	"	A. Pickett	missing		C							
	S/13085	"	P. McCall	missing		D							
	S/14442	"	R. McVey	missing		D							
	S/15723	"	J. Dunlop	missing		D							
	5206	"	J. Carrol	missing		D							
	S/15614	"	H. Park	missing		D							
	5722	"	J. Stewart	missing		D							

2nd Battalion The Queen's Own Cameron Highlanders.

Hour, Date, and Place	Summary of Events and Information	Remarks and References to Appendices
11th May Tuesday Hooge (trenches)	At daylight the sector was held as follows. A & B Companies N.E. edge of SANCTUARY WOOD. 1 Company 1/A.&S.H. thence to Cavalry trench S of HOOGE Cottages. "C" Company Camerons to Orchard. 2 Companies A.&S.H. to wood clump in Chateau Grounds. R.B. supported by 3rd K.R.R. thence to S.W. corner of BELLEWARDE Lake. D Coy was brought back into Reserve at HOOGE. About 7 a.m. an intense bombardment was opened on the N.E. corner of SANCTUARY WOOD & A & B Coys with 1 Coy A.&S.H. forced from their trenches. Rallied on their supports about 10 a.m. they were gallantly led by Capt. McCall & Lt. Anderson in a counter attack & re-occupied their trenches. Lt. Anderson was killed in the charge. The 1st Royal Scots reinforced A & B Coys & the Leinsters moved into close support.	

Casualty-List for 11th May. 1915.
K 1 + 24 W 8 + 83. M 28

Date	No	Rank	Name	Killed	Wd	Coy	Date	No	Rank	Name	Killed	Wd	Coy
11th May	S/15406	Pte	J. Allan	K		B	11th May	S/12864	Pte	J. Gowans		W	A
	S/12434	"	L. Spicer	K		B		9118	"	W. McIntosh		W	A
	S/13112	L/Cpl	A. Donaldson	K		D		9463	Sgt	J. Rankine	DofW 13/5/15		A
	6804	Pte	J. McMahon	K		B		S/15749	Pte	G. Chappell		W	A
	S/11312	Cpl	L. Adamson	K		A		9880	"	W. Calder		W	A
	9440	L/Cpl	J. McKenzie	DofW		A		S/15558	"	D. Campbell		W	A
	9219	Pte	J. McKay	K		A		8325	"	L. Ormsby		W	A
	8498	"	A. Kennedy	K		A		6756	"	H. Healey		W	A
	8360	"	D. Rogan	K		D		S/16444	"	E. Stewart		W	A
	14102	"	W. Reid	K		A		S/16238	Cpl	A. Hart		W	A
	9069	L/Cpl	W. McBain	K		A		6683	Pte	D. McInnes		W	A
	S/16630	Pte	A. McTaggart	K		A		8626	"	A. Reid		W	A
	S/15514	"	L. Fairholm	K		C		S/12441	"	W. Himlin		W	A
	8040	L/Cpl	H. Cuthbertson	K		C		9369	L/Cpl	D. McVinish		W	A
	S/16244	Pte	M. Cuthbertson	K		C		6489	L/Cpl	L. Miles		W	A
	S/15945	"	J. Gallacher	K		C		S/12466	Pte	D. Morrison		W	A
	Lt		J. R. H. Anderson	K		A		8592	"	A. Sutherland		W	A
	6925	Pte	J. Maxwell	K		B		6860	"	J. Pringle		W	A
	9091	"	A. Stewart	K		C		S/16234	"	A. Black		W	A
	16440	"	R. Nesbit	K		A		8674	"	A. Anderson		W	A
	8723	"	W. Stewart	K		A		9991	"	W. Porteous		W	C
	11344	"	A. Bryce	K		A		8900	"	A. Donegan		W	C
	15470	"	G. McLeod	K		A		8436	"	H. Connor		W	A
	9695	"	W. Nelson			A		S/5485	"	D. McVicar		W	C
	S/15562	"	D. Walker		W	B		S/5420	L/Cpl	J. McLean		W	C
	S/16549	"	R. Monteith		W	B		S/15469	Pte	J. Baxter		W	C
	12422	"	W. Locking		W	B		8713	"	A. McLean	DofW 18/5/15		C
	S/16145	"	D. McMillan		W	B		8993	"	J. Matheson		W	C
	9668	"	D. Taylor		W	B		S/16584	"	J. Reid	Cas. F.		C
	S/16438	"	P. Green		W	B		S/14423	"	J. Burr		W	C
	S/16603	"	A. Laurie		W	B		15405	"	A. Carmichael		W	C
	9641	"	J. McIntosh		W	A		S/14483	"	J. Keyte		W	C
	Capt		R. L. McCall		W	B		S/14086	"	A. Kerr		W	C
	Lt		R. A. C. Henderson		W	B		15408	"	J. Brodie		W	C
	9669	Pte	J. McDonald		W	B		6454	Sgt	J. Hendry		W	C
	8634	"	J. Balmer		W	B		8320	Pte	J. Cox		W	C
	8821	"	J. McKay		W	B		S/16651	"	W. Holbein		W	C
	9162	"	S. Anderson		W	B		9150	"	J. Park		W	C
	S/5882	"	J. Handyside		W	B		8994	"	A. Scott		W	C
	S/15092	"	H. Cameron		W	B		S/16864	"	R. Hunter		W	C
	16501	"	A. McGregor		W	A		11220	Sgt	W. Stewart		W	B
								Lieut. Col.		Campbell DSO		W	HQ

Casualty - List for 11th May 1915 [contd]

Date	No	Rank	Name	Killed	Wd.	Coy	Date	No	Rank	Name	Killed	Wd.	Coy
11th May	8983	Pte	C. Smith		W	B	11th May	16484	Pte	J. Hiddleston		missing	B
	9844	"	C. Briscoe		W	C		13634	"	J. Jack		missing	B
	16130	"	A. McLachlan		W	C		16345	"	J. Rankine		missing	B
	2/Lt	G.	S. McKay		W	C		9130	"	G. McKenzie		missing	B
	9144	Pte	R. Stewart		W	B		14010	"	D. McCallum		missing	B
	16349	"	N. McLachlan		W	C		8733	"	J. Craig		missing	C
	7004	"	J. Reid	Gas	Y	C		8384	"	M. Hammell		missing	C
	15899	"	G. McVean	Gas	Y	D		14168	"	R. Alexander		missing	C
	9863	"	P. Robertson		W	D		9642	"	J. McLachlan		missing	C
	15208	"	A. Gogarty		W	D		16388	"	G. Martin		missing	C
	6692	"	A. Whitecross		W	A		16334	"	J. Reid		missing	C
	16615	"	W. Ritchie		W	A		16233	"	R. Weems		missing	C
	15594	"	J. McPhee		W	A		8303	L/Cpl	J. Wynne		missing	D
	9450	"	J. Ross		W	A							
	9684	"	J. Reid		W	A							
	9422	"	J. Robertson		W	A							
	16484	"	J. Richardson		W	A							
	9461	L/Cpl	R. Allan		W	A							
	16532	Pte	W. Stevenson		W	A							
	16621	"	A. Bookless		W	A							
	16115	"	D. McGhee		W	B							
	16366	L/Cpl	J. Murray		W	B							
	16640	Pte	G. Bryce		W	B							
	16663	"	R. Douglas		W	B							
	6444	"	D. McIntyre		W	B							
	16661	"	R. Cairns		W	B							
	16534	"	J. Duff		W	B							
	4142	a/Cpl	W. Paterson	missing		A							
	8844	Pte	H. Chapman	missing		B							
	4424	"	A. Hulton	missing		B							
	4803	L/Cpl	J. Murray	missing		B							
	4440	"	J. Thomson	missing		B							
	13209	Pte	J. Sim	missing		B							
	13080	"	J. Anderson	missing		B							
	15856	"	J. Middlemas	missing		B							
	5810	"	O. Devine	missing		B							
	9430	"	J. Mitchell	missing		B							
	9144	"	R. Stewart	missing		B							
	16943	"	J. Brown	missing		B							
	16098	"	W. Campbell	missing		B							
	16184	"	J. Donaldson	missing		B							
	16286	"	A. Copie	missing		B							

2nd Battalion The Queen's Own Cameron Highlanders.

Hour, Date, and Place	Summary of Events and Information	Remarks and References to Appendices

12th May Wed
HOOGE
(trenches)
	'A' & 'B' Coys were relieved by 1st Royal Scots after dark & proceeded to Bde Hd Qrs in SANCTUARY WOOD where they were accommodated in dug-outs. 'C' Coy remained in support trench & 'D' Coy in reserve at Batln Hd Qrs. The Leinsters commenced a switch trench from 'C' Coy in support trench, to 1 Royal Scots in fire trenches.
	A quiet day.
	
	Casualties Killed S/10563 Pte J. Campbell B Coy
	2 S/16115 " A. Johnstone A " (wounded)
	         S/16612 " A. Clark A "
	
	Wounded 16932 Pte J. Middleton C Coy
	6 15982 " G. Cameron B "
	         7615 " G. McKay B "
	         7352 L/Cpl J. Snelson B "
	         S/15952 Pte W. Steele B "
	         9723 " J. Murty A. S.	

2nd Battalion The Queen's Own Cameron Highlanders.

Hour, Date, and Place	Summary of Events and Information	Remarks and References to Appendices
13th May, Thursday HOOGE	A quiet day. 'C' Coy still in the support trench. The Leinsters were timed to deliver a counter-attack at 11 p.m. on the N.E. corner of SANCTUARY WOOD, but the attack did not take place until 2-30 a.m. on the 13th. It was unsuccessful. 'A' & 'B' Coys constructed new dug-outs in the vicinity of Bde Hd Qrs & were shelled, losing 7 casualties. 'A' Coy 5th D.W.I. was temporarily attached to the Battn & sent to dug-outs near 'A' & 'B' Coys. Casualties <u>Wounded</u> 6 7162 Pte A. Little B. Coy. S. duty. 8765. Pte. A. Salmond C. " S. " 5366. L.C. J. Fraser B. " S. 9452. Pte. W. Lightfoot A. " S. duty 5151. " G. Donald B. " S. 716587 " J. Lockerbie B. " S.	

2nd Battalion The Queen's Own Cameron Highlanders.

Hour, Date, and Place	Summary of Events and Information	Remarks and References to Appendices
14th May, Friday HOOGE	HOOGE village & Battn Hd Qrs. were very heavily shelled. The bombardment commenced at 4. a. m. & was very severe until 6 a.m. when it gradually subsided, ceasing finally at 9. a. m. The damage done was infinitesimal — no direct hits on the Hd Qrs dug-out. The Leinsters in the evictch trench were relieved before dawn — partly by 'C' Coy & partly by the Gloucesters. After dusk 'D' Coy relieved 'C' Coy & 'C' Coy returned to the dug-outs behind Battn Hd Qrs & were held in Battn Reserve. 'A' & 'B' Coys remained in dug-outs in SANCTUARY WOOD — also 'A' Coy 5th D.L.I. Casualties Killed 9020 Pte. R. Duncan B. Coy. 16941 " A. Gray B " S. 9309 " G. Bothwell B. " Wounded 7757 Pte W. Knowles A. Coy. S. S/16613 " W. Fenton A. " S. S/10590 " A. McKenzie C. " S. S/12907 " H. McLennan D. " 7945 LC A. Duff A. " S S/12938 Pte P. Weir B. " S/10775 " H. McIntyre D. " S.I.	D of W. 16th

2nd Battalion The Queen's Own Cameron Highlanders.

Hour, Date, and Place	Summary of Events and Information	Remarks and References to Appendices
May 15th Sat. HOOGE	A quiet day. No change in disposition of the Battn. The following 4 Officers arrived on appointment to the Battn and were posted to Coys as follows. 2 Lt Melvin to 'A' Coy. 2 Lt Tucker " 'B' Coy. 2 Lt Graham " 'C' Coy. 2 Lt Moffat " 'D' Coy. They reached H.d Qrs. at BUSSEBOOM on the 15th & Battn Hd Qrs at HOOGE on the 16th. Casualties Wounded. S/15985 Pte B. McFarlane B Coy S. 2 S/215 " D. McGillivray A " S. O/r O.R. Effective Strength 11 414 Total 31 976 To Complete 20 562 Sick 4 Base 2 Strength 15	

2nd Battalion The Queen's Own Cameron Highlanders.

Hour, Date, and Place	Summary of Events and Information	Remarks and References to Appendices
May 16th, Sunday HOOGE	Capt A. D. Macpherson arrived at Hd Qrs. BUSSEBOOM & joined at Battn Hd Qrs. HOOGE on 17th - taking over command of the Battn from Capt A.C. Lampear. Our guns shelled the German trenches & the houses on the S. of the MENIN ROAD with some success during the day. The 1 Royal Scots delivered a feint attack on the N.E. corner of SANCTUARY WOOD at 8.45 p.m. They found it clear of Germans except for a few snipers. Another quiet day. Casualties Wounded (Died of Wounds)	8878 L.S.D. Fraser C. Coy.

2nd Battalion The Queen's Own Cameron Highlanders.

Hour, Date, and Place	Summary of Events and Information	Remarks and References to Appendices
May 17th Monday HOOGE	Our guns again shelled the German lines. Otherwise very quiet. Rained heavily all night. Casualties Wounded 2 S/13372 Pte W. Galloway C.Coy. S. S/15206 " W. McCahill D " S.	

2nd Battalion The Queen's Own Cameron Highlanders.

Hour, Date, and Place	Summary of Events and Information	Remarks and References to Appendices
May 18th Tues. HOOGE	The Battalion was relieved by the IX Cav. Bde. The relief was timed to take place at 10.30.p.m., but it was 2.a.m. on the 19th before "D" Coy was relieved by XIXth Hussars. The Battalion proceeded to rest camp at the X roads 1000 yds N.N.W. of HEKSKEN a distance of 11½ miles. Companies marched independently – were given tea & filled their water-bottles at the level crossing 1 mile E of YPRES, & were met by 2 motor-buses & 6 G.S. wagons at the VLAMERTINGHE level crossing. All "Come-duchi" were put in these conveyances. The last Coy marched into the bivouac at 7.30.a.m. 19th inst. Officers went into billets – Battn H.d Qrs. being at the Estaminet. The Battn had been in the trenches continuously since the 21st April & was badly in need of a rest. Capt. Donald Cameron had to report sick before the relief took place & was sent away by motor ambulance in the evening. Rained most of the night. Casualties Wounded 9651 Pte J. McKenzie A. Coy. 2 7259 " W. Blackwood A " S.	

2nd Battalion The Queen's Own Cameron Highlanders.

Hour, Date, and Place	Summary of Events and Information	Remarks and References to Appendices
May 19th, Wed. HEKSKEN X ROADS	A day of rest. Bn remained in bivouac.	

2nd Battalion The Queen's Own Cameron Highlanders.

Hour, Date, and Place	Summary of Events and Information	Remarks and References to Appendices

May 20th
HEKSKEN
X Roads.
Thursday.
	The Battalion, together with the Gloucesters, & Argylls, was inspected by Sir John French. After the inspection, which took place at 12.15 p.m., the C-in-C addressed the battalions complimenting them on the magnificent part they had played in the 2nd Battle of YPRES. He asserted that Italy's final decision to join the Allies was largely due to the gallant stand made by the British Forces before YPRES. After the address Brig: Gen: Croker, commanding the 81st Bde, called for 3 cheers for the C-in-C, & the units then returned to their bivouacs.
	The following were granted leave till the 25th inst:
	2 Lt Hunter. 'A' Coy.
	2 Lt Fraser. Transport Officer
	2 Lt Mills. 'C' Coy
	2 Lt Macleod. Machine Gun Officer
	Lt WIER. R.A.M.C.
	Rev A. Gilchrist. Chaplain.
	A composite Battn, under the command of Lt Col Kinkee of the Argylls, has been formed as under:—
	                Gloucesters 250
	                Camerons 250
	                Argylls 500
	                    Total 1000
	A fine sunny day.	

2nd Battalion The Queen's Own Cameron Highlanders.

Hour, Date, and Place	Summary of Events and Information	Remarks and References to Appendices
HEKSKEN X Roads. 21st May. Friday 1915	Bn. remained in bivouac. As on former nights heavy artillery & rifle fire heard from trenches E of YPRES & E of DANOUTRE. Fine, warm, sunny day	

2nd Battalion The Queen's Own Cameron Highlanders.

Hour, Date, and Place	Summary of Events and Information	Remarks and References to Appendices
HEKSKEN X Roads 22nd May Saturday 1915	Bn remained in bivouac. In the afternoon the baths at RENINGHELST were allotted to us & all men washed. Fine warm day.	
Effective Strength	Off 15 O.R. 515	
So late	31 976	
To complete	16 461	
Sick & missing	2 534	
base	2	
Strength	17 1051	

2nd Battalion The Queen's Own Cameron Highlanders.

Hour, Date, and Place	Summary of Events and Information	Remarks and References to Appendices
HERZEELE X Roads. 23rd May, Sunday 1915	Bn. remained in bivouac. About 5pm a draft of 78 men under 2Lt I.C. Cameron arrived of these 25 were from base details. 2Lt. Cameron temp: posted to D. Coy. Fine warm.	

2nd Battalion The Queen's Own Cameron Highlanders.

Hour, Date, and Place	Summary of Events and Information	Remarks and References to Appendices
HERSKEN X Roads to Huts N.W. YPRES. 24th May. Monday 1915	At 4 a.m. Bn received orders to be prepared to move at ½ hr notice in support of 4th & Cav. Divs in trenches in front of Hooge which had been attacked during night. Heavy firing was going on at this hour and the fumes of shell gas were most noticeable even in the bivouacs. A fairly fresh breeze was at the time blowing from the N.E. At 3.15 p.m. orders came to move at once to § H1B (8.m) The Bn marched with 1st line Transport & arrived at the huts about 7 pm. The Huts were found empty & accordingly occupied. Heavy shelling continued all day & through the night mostly from our guns. The enemy making very little reply. Lt T.A. Jones R.A.M.C. Temporarily took over duties of M.O. Fine - warm.	

2nd Battalion The Queen's Own Cameron Highlanders.

Hour, Date, and Place	Summary of Events and Information	Remarks and References to Appendices
HUTS. N.W. YPRES 25th May, Thursday 1915	& 1st A&SH & 1 R.S. Bn. occupied huts as on 24th. About 5 am Enemy's artillery opened fire on neighbouring fields obviously searching for our and French artillery which occupy several positions close by. A quiet day until 10 pm when our artillery commenced heavy firing which was kept up for about 2 hrs. Fine warm.	

2nd Battalion The Queen's Own Cameron Highlanders.

Hour, Date, and Place	Summary of Events and Information	Remarks and References to Appendices
HUTS W. of YPRES 26th May. Wednesday 1915	Bn. continued to occupy huts. During day orders received that Bn. & Gloucesters would remain in huts as Divn Reserve to 28th Divn, the remainder of 81st Bde to move back. About midnight 8th & 9th Durham L.I. (Northumbrian Divn) arrived in huttments from French line. Fine Warm.	

2nd Battalion The Queen's Own Cameron Highlanders.

Hour, Date, and Place	Summary of Events and Information	Remarks and References to Appendices
HUTS. W. of YPRES 27th May. Thurs 1915	Bn. remained in Huts in Reserve to 28th Div'n. 2nd Lt. Mills, McLeod, Fraser, & Hunter also Rev. A. Gilchrist returned from leave to U.K. & reported @ H.Q. The following officers joined for duty & were posted to Coys as under:— Capt. A. de L. Long 3/A&SH to B Coy {took over Command} Lieut. R. Campbell 3/A&SH to C " " R. Letters 3/A&SH to A " 2nd Lt. A.D. Bell-Irving 3/G.H. to C " " W.G.M. Beardmore 3/G.H. to B " " W.T. Harragin 3/G.H. to A " 2nd Lt. Mills took over duties of Adjutant from 2nd Lt. Collier. N. Wind Cold	

2nd Battalion The Queen's Own Cameron Highlanders.

Hour, Date, and Place	Summary of Events and Information	Remarks and References to Appendices
Huts W. of YPRES to LOCRE 28th May. Friday 1915	At 10.50am Bn. was relieved by Lincolns [4th Divn.] and with Gloucesters followed remainder of Brigade to LOCRE arriving there about 2pm. (7½ miles). A. Coy. billeted in YMCA quarters, remainder of Bn. bivouaced in field. Fine and fresh.	
LOCRE to STEENWERK 29th May Saturday 1915	At 5 am Bn. marched along BAILLEUL road [to starting point thence as a brigade march was continued] to bivouac 2 miles S.W. STEENWERK which was reached about 8 am. The G.O.C. Lt. Genl. Sir W.P. Pulteney(?) 3rd Corps to which the 27th Divn. has been transferred watched the Bde pass just S. of BAILLEUL. At 1 pm. Officers of the Bde went in motor busses to ARMENTIERES and thence on foot to new trenches S.E. of that place running from RUE de BOIS N.E. across LILLE road. Trenches found to be in perfect condition a huge change after those seen & held hitherto. A draft of 178 of whom 44 were men from Base – joined under 2nd Lieut Collinson(?) who was temp: posted to C Coy Fine – warm.	

2nd Battalion The Queen's Own Cameron Highlanders.

Hour, Date, and Place	Summary of Events and Information	Remarks and References to Appendices
STEENWERK TO ARMENTIERES 30th May Sunday 1915	At 5 pm the Bn. marched to billets in ARMENTIERES arriving at 7.30 pm. Route CROIX du BAC — BAC St MAUR — ERQUINGHEM LYS. The remainder of Bde less 9th R Scots took over trenches from 16th & part of 17th Bdes. ARGYLLS in right sector, GLOUCESTERS centre, 1/R Scots left sector. Camerons & 9/R Scots getting first period of rest. 10 men unable to march conveyed in Motor Ambulance. Fine fresh W wind	
ARMENTIERES 31st May Monday 1915	Bn. remained in billets. Warm fine. Total Casualties to date 28 Officers 928 O.R.	

81st Inf.Bde.
27th Div.

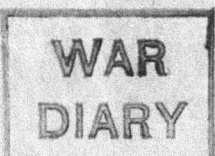

2nd BATTN. THE QUEEN'S OWN CAMERON HIGHLANDERS.

J U N E

1 9 1 5

2nd Battalion The Queen's Own Cameron Highlanders.

Hour, Date, and Place	Summary of Events and Information	Remarks and References to Appendices
ARMENTIERES 1st June Tues 1915	Bn remained in billets. Fine & warm	

2nd Battalion The Queen's Own Cameron Highlanders.

Hour, Date, and Place	Summary of Events and Information	Remarks and References to Appendices
ARMENTIERES 2nd May - Wed: 1915	Bn. remained in billets. In the afternoon CO & Coy Commdrs visited trenches held by 1/R. Scots - with Hdq. @ Pon de Biez. with a view to taking them over on the following day. Trenches in very good condition consisted almost entirely of breastworks - the ground being too low lying & wet for digging. They ran from about 100 S of LILLE road to 500 N of it on a line in front of road through CHARD'S & PIGGOTS Farms. Enemy's trenches about 200-250 yds distant - ground quite flat, rising in rear of Enemy's trenches to WEZ MACQUART. Communication trenches & support lines are numerous and good. Water in trenches plentiful. Capt R.L. McCall rejoined from No 4 Canadian Hospl Le Touquet and took over command of C. Coy. Fine Warm	

2nd Battalion The Queen's Own Cameron Highlanders.

Hour, Date, and Place	Summary of Events and Information	Remarks and References to Appendices
ARMENTIERES TO TRENCHES FARM du BIEZ 3rd June. Thurs. 1915	Bn. remained in billets until 5.20 p.m. when they commenced relief of 1/R. Scots in trenches. A, B, C. Coys took over trench line from left to right with D. Coy finding a platoon in support to each and one platoon in LILLE POST. Bn. H.Q. were @ FARM du BIEZ. Coys relieved simultaneously by three separate communication trenches. One M.G. found by 1/R. Scots was manned in Reserve trenches near CHAPELLE D'ARMENTIERES - remaining four in fire trenches. German trenches in front of sector varied from 250 to 400 yds distant. Enemy quiet - no casualties. At 7 am saw 5th K Battn. march out from NIEPPE - a fine body of men. Generally fine - some showers	

2nd Battalion The Queen's Own Cameron Highlanders.

Hour, Date, and Place	Summary of Events and Information	Remarks and References to Appendices
TRENCHES F^{nt} du BIEZ 4th June. Friday 1915	Bn. occupied Trenches. Enemy very quiet all day. Work was carried out on Wire and in plucking Grass in front of it. Also in reconnoitring all neighbouring trenches & country. No casualties. Warm - little Sun.	

2nd Battalion The Queen's Own Cameron Highlanders.

Hour, Date, and Place	Summary of Events and Information	Remarks and References to Appendices
TRENCHES F^m au BIEZ 5th June Sat. 1915	Bn. occupied trenches. Quiet day and night. Work on wire-grass and shell-proofs continued. No casualties. Warm - Sun 	Off	OR	Horses	MG	4W	2W	b
---	---	---	---	---	---	---	---
Effective Strength	24	796	76	4	21	8	3
Establishment	31	976	77	4	21	8	9
To complete	7	180	1				6
Sick & base		325					
Strength	24	1121							

2nd Battalion The Queen's Own Cameron Highlanders.

Hour, Date, and Place	Summary of Events and Information	Remarks and References to Appendices

TRENCHES
Fme du BIEZ
6th June – Sun.
1915
	Bn occupied trenches. Generally quiet. About 2 pm. some shells – "whiz-bangs" – were put over B. Coy. one bursting in trees in front of parapet wounded 1 Sgt Major and three men. A draft of 100 men arrived and were sent up to trenches 26 of these were from base.
	  Fine – warm.
	 Casualties – Wounded 1685 C.S.M. A. Douglas B Coy. S.
	         6186 Pte J. Sutherland B " S.
	         15748 " A. Seath B " S.
	         17334 " R. McGill B " S.	

2nd Battalion The Queen's Own Cameron Highlanders.

Hour, Date, and Place	Summary of Events and Information	Remarks and References to Appendices
TRENCHES FME du BIEZ 7th June - Mon. 1915	Bn. occupied trenches. About 4-30 pm and 6.30 pm enemy put over A and B Coys trenches - one burst in front of & blew in a few yards of B Coys trench. At same hour some shells came into Bn H.Q. but beyond knocking down a barn door and scattering a straw heap - did no damage. Fine - warm.	Quiet day, again at some shells

2nd Battalion The Queen's Own Cameron Highlanders.

Hour, Date, and Place	Summary of Events and Information	Remarks and References to Appendices
TRENCHES (F^m du BIEZ) TO ARMENTIÈRES 8th June Tues. 1915	Bn occupied trenches Relief by 1/R. Scots took place at 9.15 pm. C. Coy. on right being previously relieved by 2/Gloucesters at 7.30 pm. A quiet day with little firing in the early morning four stink bombs were fired at B Coy's trenches two came over parapet but caused no damage - the grass was blackened where they fell and a strong unpleasant smell remained for some time. Relief completed about 11 pm with two casualties caused by a man of 1/R Scots letting off his rifle in Cmn. trench and wounding two men. Nightly Casualties Wounded 9210 L/C J. Barrie A. Coy. accidental { 9111 Pte J. Black A "Duty 8901 Cpl J. Philip C " " Warm - generally fine - thundery. Transport moved out to fields W. of Town near canal bank.	

2nd Battalion The Queen's Own Cameron Highlanders.

Hour, Date, and Place	Summary of Events and Information	Remarks and References to Appendices
ARMENTIERES 9th June - Wed. 1915	Bn. remained in billets. At 7.30 p.m. C Coy made up to 200 by platoon A Coy. Furnished digging party for support line under direction of R.E. A.B.C Coys washed & obtained change of clothing @ baths in ERQUINGHEM-LYS. Warm - some rain	

2nd Battalion The Queen's Own Cameron Highlanders.

Hour, Date, and Place	Summary of Events and Information	Remarks and References to Appendices
ARMENTIERES 10th June Thurs. 1915	Bn. remained in billets. & 6 NCOs & men went to bus to take part in as to effect of poisonous gas. & efficacy of gas helmets & pads. - Conclusions helmet - provided it was intact - a perfect protection, the gauze face pad by no means certain protection & of little use to protect eyes. A Coy sent one platoon to work on Support trenches early morning of 11th. Fine - cloudy - warm	Three officers Bailleul by motor a demonstration

2nd Battalion The Queen's Own Cameron Highlanders.

Hour, Date, and Place	Summary of Events and Information	Remarks and References to Appendices
ARMENTIERES 11th June, Fri 1915	Bn. remained in billets. At 7.45 p.m. B. Coy. made up to 200 by 1 platoon A Coy. dug new support line of trenches just behind fire trenches - under R.E. C. Coy. relieved D. Coy. in support to 1/R. Scots - no casualties. Dull - warm	

2nd Battalion The Queen's Own Cameron Highlanders.

Hour, Date, and Place	Summary of Events and Information	Remarks and References to Appendices

ARMENTIERES
12th June. Sat.
1915
	Bn. remained in billets.
	
	Warm. Cloudy
	
	         O/f OR Ct LD HD P M MG 4W 2W B
	Effective Strength ×26 857 1 36 12 8 6 4 21 5 3
	War Estab. ×31 976 15 42 12 8 4 21 5 9
	To Complete 5 119 ✓ ✓ ✓ ✓ ✓ ✓ 6
	Sick Base 297
	Strength 26 1156 42 12 8 4 21 5 3
	
	The following NCOs & men were awarded D.C.Ms. in G.H.Q. List No. 33 d/ 12-6-15
	  No. 4314 C.S.M. G. McCallum
	  " 5175 S. J. Arthur
	  " 9740 L.Cpl. J. McKenzie (Killed)
	  " 7035 C. W. Liddell
	  " 7276 Pte. W. Rumpitt
	  " 7506 Pte. J. Nelson
		× Includes M.O. & Chaplain
		o Includes 1 Mess Cart & a hand cart
		
		B. Coy
		B. Coy
		A. Coy
		B. Coy
		D. Coy
		B. Coy

2nd Battalion The Queen's Own Cameron Highlanders.

Hour, Date, and Place	Summary of Events and Information	Remarks and References to Appendices
ARMENTIERES 13th June Sunday 1915	Bn. remained in billets. Church parade was held in the swimming baths - Bn. in billets. Warm & dull. Casualty. Wounded 15383 Pte. P. White C. Coy S.I.	

2nd Battalion The Queen's Own Cameron Highlanders.

Hour, Date, and Place	Summary of Events and Information	Remarks and References to Appendices
ARMENTIERES TO TRENCHES (Fmi du BIEZ) 14th June – Monday 1915	Bn relieved 1/R. Scots in trenches commencing 9 p.m. – relief completed 11 p.m. No casualties. Coys occupied trenches from left to right in order A.B.C.D. with C.Coy 1/R.Scots in close support – to ULCE Post. – Since last occupation 2 new trenches taken over on right – one put up on right. D. Coy & Transport – now baths. Dull – fine	

2nd Battalion The Queen's Own Cameron Highlanders.

Hour, Date, and Place	Summary of Events and Information	Remarks and References to Appendices
TRENCHES Fme de B1E2 15 June Tues 1915	Quiet day — Bn occupied trenches. Enemy put a few shells over him but without doing much damage. Warm Fine	

2nd Battalion The Queen's Own Cameron Highlanders.

Hour, Date, and Place	Summary of Events and Information	Remarks and References to Appendices
TRENCHES (Fm du Bis 2) 16th June Wed: 1915	Bn occupied trenches — all quiet. Casualty killed S/16064 Cpl G. Hutchison B. Coy. (buried CHAPPELLE D'ARMENTIERES MIL. CEMETRY) Fine — cooler Captain Donald Cameron rejoined from England, and took over command of 'A' Coy	

2nd Battalion The Queen's Own Cameron Highlanders.

Hour, Date, and Place	Summary of Events and Information	Remarks and References to Appendices
TRENCHES (F^n du BIEZ) 17th June - Thursday 1915	Bn. occupied trenches. In the evening the right trench by kts by D. Coy was handed over to Bn on right and another trench 71 and part of 72 were taken over on left of our line. A quiet day. A few "whizz-bangs" were put into C Coy trench in the afternoon without doing any damage. Fine warm. No casualties	

2nd Battalion The Queen's Own Cameron Highlanders.

Hour, Date, and Place	Summary of Events and Information	Remarks and References to Appendices
TRENCHES (Pⁿ du ZIEZ) 18th June 1915	Bn occupied trenches. A very quiet day. A certain amount of firing takes place at night, the enemy sweeping the parapet and the ground in front of it with M. Gun. Little or no damage has been effected up to date. Fine – Much Cooler – No wind No Casualties A draft of 110 NCOs & men joined the Bn. of whom 10 were from Base details. 2 Lieut C. Wilson 3/9 H posted to C. Coy. 2 Lt C.H. Turner 3/9 H " " B " arrived with it	

	Off	OR	LH	LD	HO	P	M	RG	4W	2W	k
Effective Strength	28	967	11	20	27	9	7	4	21	5	3
Estab.	31	976	15	42	12	5		4	21	5	9
To Complete	3	9					✓	✓	✓		6
Surplus			1		1			✓	✓	✓	
Sick & base		151									
Strength	28	1120									

2nd Battalion The Queen's Own Cameron Highlanders.

Gale & Polden, Ltd., Printers, Aldershot. 7,657-u.

Hour, Date, and Place	Summary of Events and Information	Remarks and References to Appendices
TRENCHES (Pm. du 31E2) 19th June Sat. 1915	Bn occupied trenches. A very quiet day no casualties. Fine — Cool	

2nd Battalion The Queen's Own Cameron Highlanders.

Hour, Date, and Place	Summary of Events and Information	Remarks and References to Appendices
TRENCHES FM du BIEZ to ARMENTIERES 20th June Sunday 1915	Bn occupied trenches until 9pm when relieved by 1/R. Scots. Relief completed by 11.30 pm. No casualties. B. Coy moved to LILLE POST (one platoon HAYSTACK FM.) in close support to 1/R. Scots. A quiet day. Fine - Cool. The following NCO & man were awarded D.C.M. in G H Q List 34. of 17-6-15 No. 6668 L. A. Douglas B. Coy " 7058 P. T. Dicketts D. Coy.	

2nd Battalion The Queen's Own Cameron Highlanders.

Hour, Date, and Place	Summary of Events and Information	Remarks and References to Appendices
ARMENTIERES 21st June. Monday 1915	Bn. remained in billets. "B" Coy in close support at LILLE POST. A.D.4½C. visited baths at ERQUINGHEM LYS. Fine Warmer	

2nd Battalion The Queen's Own Cameron Highlanders.

Hour, Date, and Place	Summary of Events and Information	Remarks and References to Appendices
ARMENTIERES 22nd June Tuesday 1915	Bn remained in billets. At 7.45 p.m. D Coy made up to 250 from A. dug on support line. Capt R Campbell 3/ASH (attached) was in charge of the party & was wounded. Casualty Wounded Capt Ronald Campbell 3/ASH. D Coy. Fine - Warm	

2nd Battalion The Queen's Own Cameron Highlanders.

Hour, Date, and Place	Summary of Events and Information	Remarks and References to Appendices
ARMENTIERES 23rd June Wed. 1915	Bn remained in billets. At 9 pm. A. Coy. relieved B. Coy. at LILLE POST & HAYSTACK FM. in close support to 1/R. Scots. Lt Col J.D. McLachlan arrived from U.K. and took over command of Battn from Capt (Temp. Major) A.E. Macpherson — who resumed the duties of Adjutant. Capt. A.C. Lampson took over comd of D. Coy. from 2/Lt R.D. Wylie. 2 platoons C. Coy. washed. Warm — Some rain.	

2nd Battalion The Queen's Own Cameron Highlanders.

Hour, Date, and Place	Summary of Events and Information	Remarks and References to Appendices

ARMENTIERES
24th June Thurs
1915
	Bn. remained in billets.
	The following officers & NCOs & men were mentioned in C in C despatch of 5-4-15
	    Maj & Bvt Lt Col. J. Campbell D.S.O.
	    Maj L.G. Graeme
	    Capt & Adjt A.D. Macpherson
	    Capt I.C. Grant
	    2 Lt J. Giffen
	    " D. Grant
	No. 6685 A/Sgt A. Douglas
	" 7033 C/Cpl. D. Liddell
	" 8084 L.C. J. Fairley
	" 9377 P. A. Hendry
	" 9179 " H.G. Hervey
	" 7162 Dr J. Little
	" 7278 L.C. S. Hoskyn (attchd Lahore Casualty Clearing Stn)
	
	Heavy rain in afternoon	

2nd Battalion The Queen's Own Cameron Highlanders.

Hour, Date, and Place	Summary of Events and Information	Remarks and References to Appendices
ARMENTIERES 26th June Fri 1915	Bn. remained in billets. The following appeared in the Gazette of 24th inst: to bear date 3/6/15 – To be C.M.G. – Maj. & Bt. Lt Col. J. Campbell D.S.O. " Brig. Major – Capt Duigh A'Macpherson Awarded Military Cross – 2/Lt J. Giffen Lt D.A. Fletcher / Cameron High arrived & was posted to A Coy. Heavy rain – warm.	

	O/R	OR	Horses & mules	RLG	4W	2W	C
Effective Strength	29	975	79	4	21	5	6
Estab	31	976	75	4	21	5	9
To Complete	2						3
Surplus		2	1				
Sick & base		106					
Strength	29	1084					

2nd Battalion The Queen's Own Cameron Highlanders.

Hour, Date, and Place	Summary of Events and Information	Remarks and References to Appendices
ARMENTIERES 26th June Sat 1915	Bn remained in billets. Orders received that owing to alteration of 3rd Corps line the relief would be postponed until 27/28 June. "B" Coy bathed & obtained change of clothing at 84 F.A. baths ERQUINGHEM - LYS. Casualty Wounded 1730 Pte R. McNeill A Coy. Fine + cooler	

H. McNary Capt

2nd Battalion The Queen's Own Cameron Highlanders.

Hour, Date, and Place	Summary of Events and Information	Remarks and References to Appendices
ARMENTIERES to TRENCHES (Pm du BIEZ) 27th June Sunday 1915	Bn relieved 1/R. Scots and 1/Argylls in trenches 65 to 68 - Coys occupying trenches from left to right A B C D. Relief commenced at 9.15 pm & was completed by 11.30 pm. No casualties. One Coy 1/R.S. in support. "Red Tickets" were received from Divl Commander for undermentioned NCOs & men to whom they were presented by C.O. No. 6668 CQMS A Douglas B. Coy " 8266 S. E Kearny A " " 7556 LC T Doherty D " " 8774 LC G Garden C " Notification was also received that the Military Cross had been awarded to Capt. R.C. McCall.	

2nd Battalion The Queen's Own Cameron Highlanders.

Hour, Date, and Place	Summary of Events and Information	Remarks and References to Appendices

TRENCHES (1m du B152) 28th June Monday 1915	Bn. occupied trenches as taken over on previous night – 3 platoons in fire trench of each Coy and 1 in support. One Coy 1/R Scots in Support – 2 platoons at LILLE POST and 2 in Subsidiary line trenches.
	
	A quiet day with little firing. Towards midnight some artillery fire was heard to North.
	
	"Green Tickets" were received from Div. Comm'd for undermentioned to whom they were given:
	   2nd Lieut Alex Fraser – Transport officer –
	   8133 Bn'dsm. W. Graham C Coy
	   8134 " J. Grant C "
	   7447 " J. Wallace C "
	
	Cloudy – cooler – some rain	

2nd Battalion The Queen's Own Cameron Highlanders.

Hour, Date, and Place	Summary of Events and Information	Remarks and References to Appendices
TRENCHES (P2 de B152) 29th June Tues 1915 Buried CHAPPELLE D'ARMENTIERES Mil. CEMETERY	Bn occupied trenches. Very quiet. Enemy put a few shells into ARMENTIERES one of which entered one of the billets of 1/R. Scots wounding 2 men. Casualties Killed No 8698 Cpl. A Cumming D Coy Wounded (accidentally) 3/6011 Pte H. Christie A " Heavy showers throughout day - cool.	9.1.

2nd Battalion The Queen's Own Cameron Highlanders.

Hour, Date, and Place	Summary of Events and Information	Remarks and References to Appendices
TRENCHES (Fm du 73162) 30th June Wed. 1915	Bn occupied trenches. A very quiet day. Casualties Wounded (accidental) No. 1/7056 Pte J. Gallie C Coy. " S/16191 Pte T. Crawford D - S.I. Cpl Cummings buried La Chapelle d'A. Rain in morning.	

81st Inf.Bde.
27th Div.

WAR DIARY

2nd BATTN. THE QUEEN'S OWN CAMERON HIGHLANDERS.

J U L Y

1 9 1 5

2nd Battalion The Queen's Own Cameron Highlanders.

Hour, Date, and Place	Summary of Events and Information	Remarks and References to Appendices
TRENCHES (Fm du BIEZ) 1st July. Thurs 1915	Re-occupied trenches. A quiet day. No casualties. Finer + Cool.	

2nd Battalion The Queen's Own Cameron Highlanders.

Hour, Date, and Place	Summary of Events and Information	Remarks and References to Appendices
TRENCHES (P.M. du BIEZ) 2nd July - Fri. 1915	Bn occupied trenches - A fairly quiet day inspite of some shelling which knocked in a few yards of trench in D. Coy. At night a little more activity was shewn but this died away, as usual, at dawn. Fine - Warm.	

2nd Battalion The Queen's Own Cameron Highlanders.

Hour, Date, and Place	Summary of Events and Information	Remarks and References to Appendices
TRENCHES (Fm du BIEZ) to ARMENTIERES 3rd July - Sat. 1915	Bn. was relieved at 9.15 pm by 1/R. Scots. Relief completed at 11 pm. One casualty. Enemy shelled other parts of our line especially to North. D. Coy remained in support to 1/R. Scots. Casualties Wounded 3/2919 Sgt H. McIver A. Coy 3/12408 Pte H. McGill B. " Fine - Warm.	

	Off	O.R.	Horses	MG	4wh	2wh	b
Effective Strength	29	971	79	4	21	5	6
Establishment	31	976	75	4	21	5	9
To Complete	2	5					3
Surplus			1				
Sick + base		95					
Strength		1066					

2nd Battalion The Queen's Own Cameron Highlanders.

Hour, Date, and Place	Summary of Events and Information	Remarks and References to Appendices
ARMENTIERES 4th July Sunday 1915	Bn less D Coy (in support to 1st R Scots) occupied billets. Church parade was held in the swimming baths. In the evening about 6 p.m. Enemy dropped several shells on ARMENTIERES - LILLE Road South of 2nd level crossing. Some houses were damaged & holes made in road otherwise little damage was done. A draft of 30 men arrived of whom 8 rejoined from base. Pipe Major Matheson was i/c of draft Fine - Warm	

2nd Battalion The Queen's Own Cameron Highlanders.

Hour, Date, and Place	Summary of Events and Information	Remarks and References to Appendices
ARMENTIERES 5th July - Mon 1915	Bn remained in billets. A fatigue party worked from 7.30 to 3 am under R.E. C. Coy bathed & obtained change of clothing at Erquinghem-Lys. Fine warm	100 men A Coy

2nd Battalion The Queen's Own Cameron Highlanders.

Hour, Date, and Place	Summary of Events and Information	Remarks and References to Appendices
ARMENTIERES 6th July - 1915	Bn remained in billets. At 9 pm C. Coy moved out to LILLE POST relieving D. Coy who returned to billets. In the afternoon B. Coy bathed. At 7.30 pm B Coy made up to 100 by A furnished a working party under R.E. Information received from Bde Hq. that D.C.M. has been awarded to No 7246 Sgt E Kearney A. Coy. for action @ Hooge on 11th May. Casualty wounded 8712 Pte T. Collijan A. Coy S.I. (unintentional) Fine - rain later - warm.	

2nd Battalion The Queen's Own Cameron Highlanders.

Hour, Date, and Place	Summary of Events and Information	Remarks and References to Appendices
ARMENTIERES 7th July - Wed. 1915	Bn remained in billets. 100 men A Coy found working party under R.E. from 9 p.m. A Coy & remainder B + transport were bathed. During this tour orders were received that all men who had only been inoculated for the first time over 6 months ago & who then only received a single dose - should be again done - this was carried out. Fine warm rain again	

2nd Battalion The Queen's Own Cameron Highlanders.

Hour, Date, and Place	Summary of Events and Information	Remarks and References to Appendices
ARMENTIERES 8th July Thurs. 1915	Bn remained in billets. About 6 p.m. several shells were fired into town and again at about 9 p.m. without however doing much damage: One "DUD" dropping in A Coy billets falling amongst cookers - no casualties. Fine - warm	

2nd Battalion The Queen's Own Cameron Highlanders.

Hour, Date, and Place	Summary of Events and Information	Remarks and References to Appendices
ARMENTIERES & TRENCHES (M du BIEZ) 9th July - Fri. 1915	Bn. relieved 1/R.Scots in trenches 65 to 68. A,B,C,D. in that order from left to right occupied trenches as on previous occasion. Relief commenced 10 pm & was completed about midnight - no casualties. C. Coy relieving from LILLE POST. Dull - windy 	

	Off	O.R.	arms	M.G	ws	eqt	b	
Effective Strength	29 x	991	78	4	21	5	6	x Includes M.O. & Chaplain
War Establt	31 x	976	78	4	21	5	9	
To Complete	2	✓	✓	✓	✓	✓	3	
Surplus		25	✓	✓	✓	✓	✓	
H... Based		103						
Strength	29	1094						

2nd Battalion The Queen's Own Cameron Highlanders.

Hour, Date, and Place	Summary of Events and Information	Remarks and References to Appendices
TRENCHES (Fm du BIEZ) 10th July Sat 1915	Bn occupied trenches with one Coy (B) of 1/R Scots in close support. 2 platoons at LILLE POST and two in subsidiary line at CHAPELLE D'ARMENTIERES. Reported that enemy has for some days been working on parapet from their front throwing up earth from trench or borrow-pit at the foot of their parapet. Draft of 11 machine gunners arrived & were posted to coys. Dull - Windy	

2nd Battalion The Queen's Own Cameron Highlanders.

Hour, Date, and Place	Summary of Events and Information	Remarks and References to Appendices
TRENCHES (Fm du B162) 11th July - Sunday 1915	Bn. occupied trenches. A quiet day - towards night about 7 Field Howitzer shells dropped in by (B Coy) without however doing any damage. Work was continued on the trenches & wiring. 2Lt S. Veitch posted to D Coy 2Lt C. Clarke " " B. arrived & were posted to coys as shewn. Dull - windy	

2nd Battalion The Queen's Own Cameron Highlanders.

Hour, Date, and Place	Summary of Events and Information	Remarks and References to Appendices
TRENCHES 12th July Mon: 1915	Bn occupied trenches. Quiet day. At nightfall the 1/R. Scots relieved them coy in close support. Enemy showed a little more activity, sniping at night & search light was in evidence until fired on by Artillery. Casualty - wounded S/16973 Pte J. Canning C. Coy. 2Lt. W. Arnot joined from Inverjordan and was posted to C Coy. Dull - cool.	

2nd Battalion The Queen's Own Cameron Highlanders.

Hour, Date, and Place	Summary of Events and Information	Remarks and References to Appendices
TRENCHES (F^m du BIEZ) 13th July Tues 1915 D of W. 13/7/15 ERQUINGHEM.	Bn. occupied trenches. About 2-30 pm Enemy registered on C. Coy (T.66) without doing any damage. Just after midnight 12/13th Lt Beardmore was hit returning from patrolling. Throughout day Enemy was observed at work on front of his parapet, also constructing dugouts &c some distance in rear. Casualties. Wounded. Lt. W. J. McBeardmore 2/gH. B Coy No 3/16533 Pte D. Blades A " Dull cool.	

2nd Battalion The Queen's Own Cameron Highlanders.

Hour, Date, and Place	Summary of Events and Information	Remarks and References to Appendices
TRENCHES (Fm du BIEZ) 14th July, W.D. 1915	Bn occupied trenches. At 8.45 pm. a Mountain Gun which had been placed in position in C Coy trench (66) opened fire on houses in WEZ MACQUART in which enemy machine guns had previously been located. Gun fire was supported by rifle & machine gun fire from our trenches which swept Enemy's parapet with a view to keeping them from observing position of gun. Considerable damage was done to houses and no M.Guns fired that night. Enemy fired a few rounds "whiz bangs" into 66 & 65 widely without doing any damage. Enemy bombarded ARMENTIERES all day - fire principally directed at MAIRIE. Some damage to house property but very few casualties. Dull - Some rain which increased to heavy downpour at night	

2nd Battalion The Queen's Own Cameron Highlanders.

Hour, Date, and Place	Summary of Events and Information	Remarks and References to Appendices
TRENCHES Fm du BIEZ to ARMENTIERES 15th July Thurs 1915	Bn. relieved by 1/R Scots at 9 p.m. relief completed 10.30 p.m. A Coy moving to LILLE POST & Subsidiary Line in close support. Generally a quiet day - though towards evening enemy put some shells into C. & B. Coy's trenches 66 & 67, knocking parapet about but without hurting anyone. Casualties Wounded S/17009 Pte G. Kennedy A. Coy 8971 " A Hardy B " Duty 5740 " G. McDonald B " S.I. Order re. alteration of Command & line received. Dull - Colder. 30 MOST men arrived of whom 6 rejoined from Base depôt.	

2nd Battalion The Queen's Own Cameron Highlanders.

Hour, Date, and Place	Summary of Events and Information	Remarks and References to Appendices
ARMENTIERES 16th July Fri. 1915	Bn remained in billets. Orders received re redistribution of line on Corps front to take effect on night 17/18th. 2/Lt. Collier proceeded on leave to U.K. 17th to 24th.	
	This Card.	

	Off.	O.R.	Horses R.g.	4 6.6	2 M.G.	b.	
Effective Strength	31 *	811	78	4	21	6	6	* Including M.O. & Chaplain
War Estab.	31 *	976	78	4	21	6	9	
To Complete	✓	55	✓	✓	✓	✓	3	
Surplus	✓	35	✓	✓	✓	✓		
Reinft base		107						
Strength		1118						

2nd Battalion The Queen's Own Cameron Highlanders.

Hour, Date, and Place	Summary of Events and Information	Remarks and References to Appendices
ARMENTIERES to CHAPELLE D'A^{mis} 17th July - Sat 1915	During the afternoon Bn. moved to new billets in CHAPELLE D'ARMENTIERES some 2000x behind french lines. Men had to be accommodated by threes & fours in small cottages. Owing to close proximity to enemy strict orders were issued as to Screening lights by night & wandering across open ground by day. A Coy were withdrawn from close support to 1/R Scots & rejoined Bn. in billets. B Coy & part of C. were bathed at ERQUINGHEM-LYS. From this night the 3/Corps to which 27th Divn together with 2nd & 15th (K. Army) Divn belongs became part of 1st Army. The 19th Bde were withdrawn from 27th Divn. 1st & 2nd Army boundary is BAILLEUL - LILLE Railway. Stormy - Wind & Rain	

2nd Battalion The Queen's Own Cameron Highlanders.

HOUR, DATE, AND PLACE	SUMMARY OF EVENTS AND INFORMATION	REMARKS AND REFERENCES TO APPENDICES
Ch. D'ARMENTIERES 18th July - Sunday 1915	Bn remained in billets - Posts told off to Companies to which they move in event of hostile arty. fire rendering billets untenable. Fine, Warm	

2nd Battalion The Queen's Own Cameron Highlanders.

Hour, Date, and Place	Summary of Events and Information	Remarks and References to Appendices
CH- D'ARMENTIERES 19? July Mon 1915	Bn remained in billets. Relaxation of C Coy into A & D. bathed at Erquinghem — A quiet day with little shelling. Capt & 9/mr D Macdonald proceeded on leave to U.K. 20th to 25th. Windy & Dusty — Cool	

2nd Battalion The Queen's Own Cameron Highlanders.

Hour, Date, and Place	Summary of Events and Information	Remarks and References to Appendices
CH-D'ARMENTIERES 20th July Tues. 1915	Bn. remained in billets. A quiet day. D. Coy. furnished a working party 150 men at 7.30 pm under R.E.	

Windy & dusty - Cool

2nd Battalion The Queen's Own Cameron Highlanders.

Hour, Date, and Place	Summary of Events and Information	Remarks and References to Appendices
CH: D'ARMENTIERES to TRENCHES (F^{me} du BIEZ) 21st July - Wed 1915	At 5 am anti aircraft — motor mount battery, entered billet area & fired on German aeroplane. After about 10 minutes enemy replied with shrapnel & whiz bangs breaking some windows without doing further damage. At 8.30 pm Bn relieved 1/R Scots — C, D, B Coys in fire trenches 10-0-10. A Coy in support in subsidiary line. A quiet night. 2/Lt W. Roberts arrived from Rouen & was posted to B Coy. Wind + dust + cool.	

2nd Battalion The Queen's Own Cameron Highlanders.

Hour, Date, and Place	Summary of Events and Information	Remarks and References to Appendices
TRENCHES A.2 & B.1 & 2 2nd July Thurs 1915	Bn occupied trenches. A quiet day. Very little shelling Showery – Cool – heavy rain to night	

2nd Battalion The Queen's Own Cameron Highlanders.

Hour, Date, and Place	Summary of Events and Information	Remarks and References to Appendices
TRENCHES Fm du BIEZ 22nd July 1915	Bn occupied trenches. Very quiet day. In afternoon own Arty: fired two or three salvos at F^m LA FLEUR D'ECOSSE Very heavy rain all day - cool	

	M/H	O.R.	Horses	M.G.				
Effective Strength	32	1002	78	4	21	6	6	Inclusive M.O. & Chaplain
War Establishment	31	976	78	4	21	6	4	
To Complete							3	
Surplus	1	26						
Sick + Base		116						
Strength	32	1118						

2nd Battalion The Queen's Own Cameron Highlanders.

Hour, Date, and Place	Summary of Events and Information	Remarks and References to Appendices
TRENCHES (Fm du BIEZ) 24th July Sat 1915	Bn occupied trenches. Very quiet day — a little more activity than usual shewn by enemy snipers & machine guns by night. Heavy cannonading heard to the north about 9.30 pm & again towards dawn on 25th. Showery — cool.	

2nd Battalion The Queen's Own Cameron Highlanders.

Hour, Date, and Place	Summary of Events and Information	Remarks and References to Appendices
TRENCHES (Fm du BIEZ) 25th July Sunday 1915	Bn occupied trenches. Quiet except for some shelling by enemy & our artillery at each other. 2Lt A.H. Collier returned from leave to U.K. Heavy rain all day.	Generally

2nd Battalion The Queen's Own Cameron Highlanders.

Hour, Date, and Place	Summary of Events and Information	Remarks and References to Appendices
TRENCHES (Ftn du BIEZ) 26th July Mon 1915	Bn occupied trenches. In afternoon enemy commenced shelling Arty: positions & observation stations in neighbourhood of our learning Subsidiary line. One shell presumably a premature burst hit two men of M Gun Section in PARADISE ALLEY. both badly hurt. Again at night probably owing to noise made by some unit relieving (possibly Northumbrian Divn on our left) they put some heavy shrapnel over road leading to Dumping Ground. Casualties Wounded 8768 Pte A. Salmond M.G.(S) Died of Wounds. 8834 Sgt H. Fraser M.G.(S) Dull - Some rain	

2nd Battalion The Queen's Own Cameron Highlanders.

Hour, Date, and Place	Summary of Events and Information	Remarks and References to Appendices
TRENCHES (F^m du BIEZ) to CH. D'ARMENTIERES 27th July. Tues. 1915	Bn. relieved at 9 pm by 1/R Scots. Relief completed 11 pm - one casualty. Some shelling by both sides during day but trenches not touched. Only one shell coming near HQ dug-out in Subsidiary line. In the afternoon our Howitzer battery shelled enemy's trenches in front of 65 with considerable accuracy. This is probably the last time the Bn. occupies this section of the Div^l. Trench line, it being intended that 81 Bde should be relieved by 80th Bde in a week's time & then after a fortnight in Divⁿ Reserve that it should relieve 82nd Bde on section of line S. of RUE de BOIS. Casualty. DIED of wounds. S/17349 Pte J. Linton D. Coy.	Fine but showery. Divisional Band was formed.

A.C. Mactavish
Capt

2nd Battalion The Queen's Own Cameron Highlanders.

Hour, Date, and Place	Summary of Events and Information	Remarks and References to Appendices
CH- D'ARMENTIERES 28th July - Wed. 1915	Bn remained in billets. Orders received that 2/Lt Harrigan and Wilson 3/H were to proceed to join 1/Gordon Highrs and that 2/Lt. Bell-Irving 3/QH was to report to GOC. R Flying Corps @ G.H.Q. These officers left for BAILLEUL in the afternoon. A working party under R.E. of 100 B Coy, 100 C Coy & 58 D Coy paraded at 8.30pm for work on CWa breastwork to fire trench. At 8.30pm Rev. G.S.J. Gilchrist buried Pte Linton in C d'A Military Cemetary. 4 men were sent to Threshing Coy. Captain & Mn D Macdonald returned from leave to U.K. Fine — warm	

2nd Battalion The Queen's Own Cameron Highlanders.

Hour, Date, and Place	Summary of Events and Information	Remarks and References to Appendices
2H - D'ARMENTIERES 29th July - Thurs. 1915	Bn remained in billets. About 8.30 am enemy put some shells into N.W. end of billets occupied by A & B Coys. No casualties. Later in the afternoon several H.E. shrapnel were put over ARMENTIERES causing some casualties. Casualty Wounded T.3181 Pte A. Pickett C. Coy. (S) Fine warm	
CH - D'ARMENTIERES 30th July - Friday 1915	Bn remained in billets. Working parties 100 A & 100 B dug on new breastwork and trenches from 8.30 pm. Fine warm	

2nd Battalion The Queen's Own Cameron Highlanders.

Hour, Date, and Place	Summary of Events and Information	Remarks and References to Appendices
CHAPELLE D'ARMENTIERES 31st July - Saturday, 1915	Bn remained in billets, bathed at Erquinghem. Commencing at 6.20 p.m. & continuing at intervals until 10 pm the Artillery of the 27th Division shelled the enemy's trenches & tmc. trenches in neighbourhood of RUE DE BOIS. The 2/Gloucester Regt & 9th R Scots combined Inn fire attack with m gun rifle & trench mortar & rifle grenade fire. Owing to possible reprisal, the Bn moved out of billets, Coys occupying trenches in the neighbourhood which afforded better protection from shell fire. Enemy replied with artillery fire but not in great volume, without doing any damage. Fine - cool	The whole Bn

81st Inf.Bde.
27th Div.

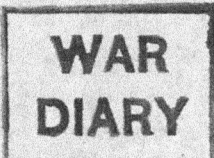

2nd BATTN. THE QUEEN'S OWN CAMERON HIGHLANDERS.

A U G U S T

1 9 1 5

2nd Battalion The Queen's Own Cameron Highlanders.

Hour, Date, and Place	Summary of Events and Information	Remarks and References to Appendices
CHAPELLE D'ARMENTIERES 1st Aug. Sunday 1915	Bn remained in billets. Enemy fired a few rounds at our artillery close round billets. Voluntary Church Parade in Yard of Brasserie - H.Q. billet. Windy + dusty	

2nd Battalion The Queen's Own Cameron Highlanders.

Hour, Date, and Place	Summary of Events and Information	Remarks and References to Appendices
CH D'ARMENTIERES to ERQUINGHEM-LYS 2nd Aug. Mon 1915	Starting at 2 pm by companies to camp about 400 yds N. of ERQUINGHEM bridge. Two huts were allotted to each Coy, the remainder of the men bivouaced in the field. Bn HQ & HQ of all Coys except C. were billeted in the village. Remainder of Bde. also in camp or billeted in farms in the neighbourhood. Bde HQ also moved from CH D'ARMENTIERES to ERQUINGHEM-LYS. The 8th M Bde who previously occupied this camp moved to the trench line held by 77th Bde. Strong wind, very dusty.	

2nd Battalion The Queen's Own Cameron Highlanders.

Hour, Date, and Place	Summary of Events and Information	Remarks and References to Appendices
ERQUINGHEM 3rd Aug 1915	In Divisional Camp. Classes in M. Gun, Bombing, Range finding were started. Coys occupied in drilling, handling arms & musketry. A Grenadier Coy 5 NCO & 60 men under Lt Mills was formed with the object of specializing men in bombing & trench mortar work. Lt R.D. Wyke proceeded on leave to U.K. from 3rd to 10th. Dull & wet. Cool.	

2nd Battalion The Queen's Own Cameron Highlanders.

Gale & Polden, Ltd., Printers, Aldershot. 1043.-w.

Hour, Date, and Place	Summary of Events and Information	Remarks and References to Appendices
ERQUINGHEM 4th Aug. Wed. 1915	Bn. remained in camp. Transport moved to field near L'EPINETTE where remainder of Bde transport was in camp. Drill continued.	
	Floncney-Warmen	
4th Aug 5th		

2nd Battalion The Queen's Own Cameron Highlanders.

Hour, Date, and Place	Summary of Events and Information	Remarks and References to Appendices
FRYVINGHEM 5th Aug. Thurs 1915	Bn. remained in Camp. Drill & route marches continued. Capt R.L. M'Call proceeded on leave to U.K. from 5th to 13th. No 7857 Cpl W Wallace left to attend a Trench Mortar Course. Fine Warm.	

2nd Battalion The Queen's Own Cameron Highlanders.

Gale & Polden, Ltd., Printers, Aldershot. 1043.-w.

Hour, Date, and Place	Summary of Events and Information	Remarks and References to Appendices
ERQUINGHEM 6th Aug. Friday 1915	Bn remained in Camp. Weather Fine Following officers appeared in Gazette d/ GHQ 6/7/15 Lt R. Pettier - Temp. Captain d/ 27/5/15 2 Lt C.M. Mills " Lieut d/ 3/5/15 " J.D. McLeod - " " d/ 4/5/15 (Lt R.D. Wylie - Temp. Captain d/ 2nd June 15 (Authy 27 Divn d/7/15/15 + 2L Bde 1008 d/5/7/15)	

2nd Battalion The Queen's Own Cameron Highlanders.

Hour, Date, and Place	Summary of Events and Information	Remarks and References to Appendices
ERQUINGHEM 7th Aug. Sat. 1915	Bn remained in Camp. Capt A.C. Lampson & Lt Fletcher proceeded on leave to UK from 7th to 15th. Warm Windy Dust	

2nd Battalion The Queen's Own Cameron Highlanders.

Hour, Date, and Place	Summary of Events and Information	Remarks and References to Appendices
ERQUINGHEM 8th Aug. Sunday 1915	Bn. remained in Camp. Divine Services held in Camp. No. 8774 L/C. Garden M.G. awarded D.C.M. Warm - Fine	

2nd Battalion The Queen's Own Cameron Highlanders.

Hour, Date, and Place	Summary of Events and Information	Remarks and References to Appendices
ERQUINGHEM 9th Aug. Mon. 1915	Bn. remained in Camp. Capt Coay & Lt Roberts & 4 NCOs detailed to superintend construction of defensive post @ LA VESÉE	

2nd Battalion The Queen's Own Cameron Highlanders.

Hour, Date, and Place	Summary of Events and Information.	Remarks and References to Appendices
ERQUINGHEM 10th Aug Thur 1915	Bn remained in Camp. Sixty men in two reliefs of 30 worked on position at LA VESEE from 9 to 4 pm. "A" Coy" attached to RE for work for one month. Casualty Wounded 9789 L/C D. McLeod A Coy. S.I. (attempted suicide) Warm - Fine.	

2nd Battalion The Queen's Own Cameron Highlanders.

Hour, Date, and Place	Summary of Events and Information	Remarks and References to Appendices
ERQUINGHEM 11th Aug. 1915	Bn remained in Camp. 160 men in two reliefs worked on post at LA VESÉE from 9.30 - 4 pm. Warm - Windy - Dust	

2nd Battalion The Queen's Own Cameron Highlanders.

Hour, Date, and Place	Summary of Events and Information	Remarks and References to Appendices
ERQUINGHEM 12th Aug. Thurs 1915	Bn remained in Camp. Lt Col McLachlan & Maj Macpherson visited new trenches 58-55 held by 1/R.I. Regt. S. of Rue de Bois. 100 men in two reliefs worked on LA VESÉE Post. Warm - Fine	

2nd Battalion The Queen's Own Cameron Highlanders.

Hour, Date, and Place	Summary of Events and Information	Remarks and References to Appendices
ERQUINGHEM 13th Aug. 1915	Bn remained in Camp. 100 men in two reliefs as on previous days worked on LA VESÉE defenses. Capt. McCall returned from leave to U.K. Draft of 20 men arrived reported to Coys (10 of these from Base) Warm – Fine	

	Off	OR	Horses	Rg	GNS	SAA	b
Effective Strength	27	985	79	4	21	6	6
Attached	1	1					
War Establishment	30	1001	70	4	21	6	9
To Complete	2	15					3
Surplus			1				
Attached	1	1					
Sick & absent	1	109					
Strength	28	1095					

Attached other units — Off / OR:
Gas Coy GHQ — 4
3/Corps Workshop — 4
27 Div Train — 5
D/E 17th Coy RE Tunnellers — 6
Short leave — 3, 8
Bomb School — —
Salvage Coy — 2
M.G. Class — 1
2 Lt H.Q. — 1
— — 1
Telephone Course — —
27 Div Tournai — —

+ Chaplain, + Sgt Cameron MPS
— M.O, # Tow. Guard.

2nd Battalion The Queen's Own Cameron Highlanders.

Hour, Date, and Place	Summary of Events and Information	Remarks and References to Appendices
ERQUINGHEM 14th Aug. Sat. 1915	Bn. remained in Camp. 160 men in two reliefs as before worked on LA VESÉE defences. Orders received to cease work in this place after today. 2/Lt J. R. Napier rejoined & was posted to "C" Coy. Cold. Windy — Dull.	

2nd Battalion The Queen's Own Cameron Highlanders.

Hour, Date, and Place	Summary of Events and Information	Remarks and References to Appendices
ERQUINGHEM 15th Aug Sunday 1915	Bn remained in Camp. Divine Service cancelled owing to rain. Capt R. Longford & Lt. Fletcher returned from leave to UK. Heavy Thunderstorms - fine later	

2nd Battalion The Queen's Own Cameron Highlanders.

Hour, Date, and Place	Summary of Events and Information	Remarks and References to Appendices
ERQUINGHEM TO TRENCHES (Sq I20 B70) 16th Aug. Monday 1915	Bn paraded for inspection by G.O.C. III Corps Lt Gen Sir W.P. Pulteney KCB, DSO at 11.45 a.m. B, C, D Coys bathed. Bn relieved 1/R. Irish in trenches 58 - 56 & Cambridgeshire Regt int 55. Relief commenced 6.15 pm & was completed by 10.30 pm. No casualties. Trenches in good order - all breast work & similar in construction & design to those held previously in left sector of Divisional line. Coys took over from right to left D.C.B.A. Bn HQ & 2 Platoons D in dugouts in rear of 58. Two M Guns with teams of 1/R. Scots attached to Bn. 82nd Bde whom 81 Bde relieved moved into Camps by Corps at ERQUINGHEM. Bn. Camps taken over by D.C.L.I. Sgt J. Cameron M.M.P. who had been attached to A Coy since 25th May - gazetted 2/Lt & posted to 2 Bn - posted to A Coy. AG 175 31st July. Thunder & very heavy rain	

2nd Battalion The Queen's Own Cameron Highlanders.

Gale & Polden, Ltd., Printers, Aldershot. 1043.-w.

Hour, Date, and Place	Summary of Events and Information	Remarks and References to Appendices
TRENCHES 17th Aug. Thurs 1915	Bn. occupied trenches as taken over on 16th. Orders received that when Bde held trenches all M.Guns would be under Bde control — not at all a satisfactory arrangement from OC Battalion's point of view, they being responsible for Sector allotted to them having now a Junior Staff officer butting in directing principal defences in their line. Difficulty also arisen as to clearing wounded, Field Ambulances claiming that it is not within their scope of duty to clear Regimental Aid Posts !!! Casualty Wounded 9/17347 Pte A. Peart A Coy (B) Thunder and Rain	

2nd Battalion The Queen's Own Cameron Highlanders.

Hour, Date, and Place	Summary of Events and Information	Remarks and References to Appendices
Trenches 15th May. W.E. 1915	Bn. breakfast trenches. Alterations in line again to H. Plan. 7 Gloucester Regt. taken over two trenches from left on right making 3 Bns and ½ R Scots in trenches and 1 Bn and ½ R Scots in support. Artillery Officer 46th Batt. comes up each night & sleeps at Bn Hq. & ret. in liaison officer. Casualty. Wounded 7459 Pte T Smith A Coy.	

2nd Battalion The Queen's Own Cameron Highlanders.

Hour, Date, and Place	Summary of Events and Information	Remarks and References to Appendices
TRENCHES 19th Aug. Thurs 1915	Bn occupied trenches. Our Artillery somewhat more active in this present sector than in that held opposite CHAPELLE D'ARMENTIERES. Germans on the other hand appear to fire less, and never at night. Our transport continues to be heard very plainly on pavé roads in rear. Casualties: Wounded (remained) 3/ no 1711 A. Knight C.oy S.I.	

2nd Battalion The Queen's Own Cameron Highlanders.

Gale & Polden, Ltd., Printers, Aldershot. 1043.-w.

Hour, Date, and Place	Summary of Events and Information	Remarks and References to Appendices
TRENCHES 26th Aug. Friday 1915	Bn. occupied trenches. CO & night [illegible] [illegible] 1/Argyll & Sutherland Highr's trenches 51-52-53 – the line to be taken over under present arrangement on the 30th inst. Casualty Wounded 11870 Pte S. Paul D Coy (Duty) 2Lt Tucker proceeded on leave to UK 20th–27th Aug.	

Fine – Cool.

	Off.	O.R.	Horses	M.G.	4 W.	2 W.	
Effective Strength	29	996	79	4	21	6	6
Attached	1	1					
War Estab.	30	1001	78	4	21	6	9
To complete	–	4		–	–	–	3
Surplus			1				
Attached	1						
Sick horses [illegible]		89					
Strength		1056					

1 Chaplain

Attached to other units		
Cadet School G.H.Q.		1
Gas Coy		4
III Corps Workshop		4
27th Div. Train		5
171 & 173 Coy R.E.		6
Short leave		2
Bomb School		
Tunnelling Coy 27 Div.		2
M.G. Class		1
Div. H.Q.		3
[illegible]		1
Bde. H.Q.		4
Works Coy R.E.	1	1
[illegible]		2
Telephone [illegible]		1
27 Div. Band		
	1	47

Adjt Maj [illegible]
[illegible]

2nd Battalion The Queen's Own Cameron Highlanders.

Gale & Polden, Ltd., Printers, Aldershot. 1043.-w.

Hour, Date, and Place	Summary of Events and Information	Remarks and References to Appendices
TRENCHES 21st Aug 1915	Bn. in field trenches. 2/Lt Mitton proceeded on leave to UK 21st-25th Aug. Casualties killed 7925 L/C R. Campbell A Coy	A quiet day.

2nd Battalion The Queen's Own Cameron Highlanders.

Hour, Date, and Place	Summary of Events and Information	Remarks and References to Appendices
TRENCHES	In occupied trenches. A quiet day. Lt Campbell's body was buried in cemetery at foot of PARK Row. Line trench J.9.b.w.	Fine. Warmer. Cool @ night.

2nd Battalion The Queen's Own Cameron Highlanders.

Hour, Date, and Place	Summary of Events and Information	Remarks and References to Appendices
TRENCHES 23rd Aug. noon 1915	Bn. relieved by 1/R Scots commencing at 8 pm - relief completed at 10.50 pm. No casualties. Bn. moved into huts on Rue Des Chavattes - Coy. & Bn. H.Q. in huts & billetted in farms. 2/Lt. S.R. Napier to Hosp. During time down in the trenches very little offensive action was taken by Enemy in trenches opposite. Some difficulty was experienced by our patrols moving between the trenches at night owing to the bright moonlight which, by reason of the fact that moon was behind German line, disclosed our action more than those of Enemy. Considerable work was carried out in improving parapets, parados & communication trenches. 2/Lt Graham Proceeded on leave to U.K. 23rd - 30th. Fine weather.	

2nd Battalion The Queen's Own Cameron Highlanders.

Gale & Polden, Ltd., Printers, Aldershot. 1043.-w.

Hour, Date, and Place	Summary of Events and Information	Remarks and References to Appendices
HUTS (RUE DELETTRES) 24 Aug 1915	Battalion in Bde reserve in Huts. Working & carrying parties of 340 men were found during day and night. 2Lt J. Cameron proceeded on leave to UK 24th – 31st Aug. Transport inspected by DMTO. Finer cool	
[illegible] 1915		

2nd Battalion The Queen's Own Cameron Highlanders.

Hour, Date, and Place	Summary of Events and Information	Remarks and References to Appendices
HUTS 24th Aug 1915	Bn. remained in Huts. Working & carrying parties 310 men furnished.	

Fine Warm

2nd Battalion The Queen's Own Cameron Highlanders.

Hour, Date, and Place	Summary of Events and Information	Remarks and References to Appendices
HUTS 26th Aug Thurs 1915	Bn. furnished six Huts & carrying parties 310. Capt Long proceeded to le from 26th Aug. to 2nd Sept. Sunny - Warm.	Working men furnished O.K. on leave

2nd Battalion The Queen's Own Cameron Highlanders.

Hour, Date, and Place	Summary of Events and Information	Remarks and References to Appendices
HUTS. 27th Aug. Friday 1915	Bn. Remained in Huts. Bn. found bathing & company parties 360 men. 2/Lt. Moffat proceeded O.K. from 27th Aug to	The whole Working party were furnished with leave to 8th Sept.
	The following appeared in Gazette. Conferred on :— Maj. B. N. W. J. Campbell CMG. DSO. — Order Class With Swords. No. 8774 L/C. G. Garden — Cross of St No. 8432 Sgt. A. McIntyre — Medal of S/14458 Pte D.S. Cameron — Medal of	of Russian decoration. of St STANISLAS 3rd GEORGE 4th Class. St GEORGE 1st Class. St GEORGE 4th Class.

2nd Battalion The Queen's Own Cameron Highlanders.

Hour, Date, and Place	Summary of Events and Information	Remarks and References to Appendices
HUTS 28th Aug. Sat. 1915	Bn. remained in huts. S/Lt Tucker returned from leave. 240 men were provided for working parties under R.E. Fine. Warm. rain @ night.	

2nd Battalion The Queen's Own Cameron Highlanders.

Gale & Polden, Ltd., Printers, Aldershot. 1043.-w.

Hour, Date, and Place	Summary of Events and Information	Remarks and References to Appendices
HUTS 29th Aug. Sunday 1915	Bn remained in Huts 340 men were provided R.C. Divine Service held in Rain + wind	for work under Field of B Coy.

2nd Battalion The Queen's Own Cameron Highlanders.

Hour, Date, and Place	Summary of Events and Information	Remarks and References to Appendices
HUTS (RUE de LETTRE) To TRENCHES (BOIS GRENIER) 30th Aug 1915	Bn. relieved 1/A.&S.H. in trenches 53-52-51. A.C.D. Coys occupying trenches in that order. B Coy moved to billets in Bde Reserve. Relief commenced at 7.45 & was completed by 9.15 pm. No casualties. Trenches all breastwork as before with a splinter proof line & support line in rear. The trenches themselves well supplied with dug out accommodation, in most places there are three rows. Condition generally good & fairly clean - wire poor. Water obtained for drinking from WATER FME about 200x in rear of 52. Bn HQ in dug outs behind support line. As at present - indications Bn holds these trenches for 14 days continuously. 2Lt Mathew returned from leave & taken over day. Windy - dull. Cold	

2nd Battalion The Queen's Own Cameron Highlanders.

Hour, Date, and Place	Summary of Events and Information	Remarks and References to Appendices
TRENCHES (BOIS GRENIER) 31st Aug Tues 1915	Bn. occupied trenches. A quiet day spent in going round & deciding on work to be done. In afternoon Major Sutton O.C. 1st Wessex F.C. R.E. came up & asked for working parties for wiring support & comm. trenches stating that work was urgently required - if necessary at the expense of other work on the trenches. This was arranged for. 2Lt Graham returned from leave. Our Artillery registering all day. Heavy rain - cold	

81st Inf.Bde.
27th Div.

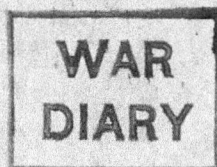

2nd BATTN. THE QUEEN'S OWN CAMERON HIGHLANDERS.

SEPTEMBER

1 9 1 5

2nd Battalion The Queen's Own Cameron Highlanders.

Gale & Polden, Ltd., Printers, Aldershot. 1043.-w.

Hour, Date, and Place	Summary of Events and Information	Remarks and References to Appendices
TRENCHES (BOIS GRENIER) 1st Sept - Wed 1915	Bn occupied trenches. At 8 pm B. Coy from Bde Reserve came up & took over T.50 from 2/Gloucester Regt. who were withdrawn to Bde Reserve after handing over this trench and T.49 & T.48 to 24th Bde. (Lincolnshire Regt) and leaving one Coy in Support in BOIS GRENIER line. 2 Lt J Cameron returned from leave. Our Artillery continued to register all day. Very wet & cold	

2nd Battalion The Queen's Own Cameron Highlanders.

Hour, Date, and Place	Summary of Events and Information	Remarks and References to Appendices
TRENCHES (BOIS GRENIER) 2nd Sept. Thurs 1915	Bn occupied trenches - Owing to heavy & continuous rain condition of trenches became very bad. At 2 am a dug out occupied by L/C Horsburgh & regimental police collapsed owing to rain - a broken beam pinning Pte Robertson to the ground. Ten minutes were taken in releasing him, by which time he was dead. Casualties Killed (Accidental) 7953 Pte J. Robertson A Coy, Wounded 17245 Pte J. Ingram C Coy (S) Duty. Continuous rain & wind - Cold. Trench Mortar fire from T.52 with some effect - Our artillery kept up constant fire throughout day. Capt Cory returned from leave	Buried in Cemetery H 20 6.7.9.

2nd Battalion The Queen's Own Cameron Highlanders.

HOUR, DATE, AND PLACE	SUMMARY OF EVENTS AND INFORMATION	REMARKS AND REFERENCES TO APPENDICES
TRENCHES (BOIS GRENIER) 3rd Sept. Fri. 1915	Bn occupied trenches. Owing to rain practically no work could be continued - great difficulty being experienced even in moving along the trenches owing to slipperyness. Our artillery continued to fire (registering) all day. In the evening enemy replied with some field guns & field howitzers on to T.5.3 & T.52. No damage done. 2/Lt Napier reported for duty from Hosp'l (Steenwerck). Heavy & continuous Rain - Cold	

	Off	OR	Horses	R.G	Mach Gun	B		Attached to Other Units	O.	OR
Effective Strength	29	952	75	4	21	6	6	Cadet School GHQ		2
Attached	1	1					M.O. & Arm'r	Gas Coy		4
War Estab.	30	1001	75	4	21	6	9	3 Corps Workshop		4
To Complete		17					3	27 Div. Train		5
Attached	1						Chaplain	171-172 Coy R.E.		6
Sick & absent	1	89						Short leave	2	8
Strength	31	1073						Bomb School	1	11
								Salvage Coy		2
								Div. H.Q.		3
								" Arm		1
								Bde H.Q.		8
								Worcs R.E.	1	2
								G.H.Q.		2
								Included in X	4	56

2nd Battalion The Queen's Own Cameron Highlanders.

Hour, Date, and Place	Summary of Events and Information	Remarks and References to Appendices
TRENCHES (BOIS GRENIER) 4th Sept. Sat. 1915	Bn occupied trenches. Day fine up to 11 am when rain commenced & continued all day, preventing any work being done. Our artillery continued to register drawing some fire from enemy guns. 7/L. Moffat returned from leave	Heavy continuous rain Thunder &c

2nd Battalion The Queen's Own Cameron Highlanders.

Hour, Date, and Place	Summary of Events and Information	Remarks and References to Appendices
TRENCHES (BOIS GRENIER) 5th Sept Sunday 1915	Bn occupied trenches. Our Artillery as usual fired all day on different portions of enemy's line. A Trench Mortar under R.G.A was placed in T.52 and fired about 12 rounds - most of which appeared to take effect. Enemy retaliated with "Sausages" & "whiz-bangs" without doing much damage. Enemy Aeroplane appeared in the evening & caused two of ours - presumably unarmed - to fly back to our line. Casualty Killed 17222 Pte R. Somerville B Coy Wounded 4850 Sgt Piper D. Matheson A Coy - Duty. Heavy rain, & cold	

2nd Battalion The Queen's Own Cameron Highlanders.

Hour, Date, and Place	Summary of Events and Information	Remarks and References to Appendices
TRENCHES (Bois Grenier) To Huts - Rue delattre 6th Sept Mon 1915	Bn. was relieved by 1/A&SH at 7.45 pm relief completed without casualties about 9.45 pm. Coys moved to billets in huts formerly occupied in Rue de lattre. This relief was unexpected as it was understood Bn. would remain in these trenches until Bde went into Div. Reserve on 13th. Artillery fire continuous all day principally by our guns with occasional reply by enemy. The first day without rain since occupying this line. Fine - cold.	

2nd Battalion The Queen's Own Cameron Highlanders.

Hour, Date, and Place	Summary of Events and Information	Remarks and References to Appendices
HUTS (Rue de Lettres) 7th Sept. Tues. 1915	Bn remained in Huts - 500 men A C D Coys bathed. 160 men furnished as working party under R.E. Fine - cool.	

2nd Battalion The Queen's Own Cameron Highlanders.

Hour, Date, and Place	Summary of Events and Information	Remarks and References to Appendices
HUTS (Rue de Lettrey) 7th Sept Wed 1915	Bn. remained in Huts. 250 men furnished as working parties under R.E. Reinforcement of 20 men arrived of whom 1 came from Base detail. C.S.M. McCallum was i/c of party. 2/Lt Wimot returned to Regt duty from attachment to Wessex R.E. — 2/Lt Napier taking his place. Fine – Cool	

2nd Battalion The Queen's Own Cameron Highlanders.

Hour, Date, and Place	Summary of Events and Information	Remarks and References to Appendices
HUTS TO TRENCHES (LA VESÉE) 9th Sept Thurs 1915	Bn remained in huts till relief of 1/RS in trenches. 350 men B Coy & details bathed. Relief of 1/RS commenced at 7.30 pm & was completed by 9.50 pm. No casualties. Coys took over trenches formerly occupied A B C D occupying 58·57·56·55 respectively – D Coy having 1 platoon @ Bn H.Q. Fine - warm	

2nd Battalion The Queen's Own Cameron Highlanders.

HOUR, DATE, AND PLACE	SUMMARY OF EVENTS AND INFORMATION	REMARKS AND REFERENCES TO APPENDICES
TRENCHES (LA-VESÉE) 10th Sept 1915	Bn occupied trenches. At 10am C.O. Adjt & Coy Commdrs 9th Yorkshire Regt (by Bde - 2nd Div) visited trenches. In the evening 7 Coys came up & were distributed 2 platoons to each trench. The test of H.E. shells which was ordered to take place was postponed.	by our Artillery take place

Effective Strength — S/O 29, O.R 1009, Horses 78, M.G. 4, 4 wh 21, 2 wh 4, cycles 6

Attached to other units & CP.
Cadet School — 2
Gas Coy, G.H.Q — 4
3rd Corps Workshop — 4
27 Div Train — 5
171-181 Coy R.E. — 25
...
Bde H.Q.
Russian R.E. — 1
A.M.P — 1
M.M.P — 1
27 Div Base

# 2nd Battalion The Queen's Own Cameron Highlanders.

Gale & Polden, Ltd., Printers, Aldershot. 1043.-w.

HOUR, DATE, AND PLACE	SUMMARY OF EVENTS AND INFORMATION	REMARKS AND REFERENCES TO APPENDICES
TRENCHES (LA DESÉE) 11th Sept 1915	Bn occupied trenches. The test of HE shells arranged for on 10th took place & the guns firing @ regular intervals throughout day. At 7.15 pm the two other coys of 4th Yorkshire Regt. & M.G. relieved the 2 coys in trenches, and these with Bn HQ went back to their billets. 2/Lt McIvor 1/R Scots who was conducting a Yeomanry M. Gun officer round trenches was killed by shell splinter. Fine - Warm	

2nd Battalion The Queen's Own Cameron Highlanders.

Hour, Date, and Place	Summary of Events and Information	Remarks and References to Appendices
TRENCHES (LA VESÉE) 12th Sept Sunday 1915	Bn occupied trenches again. Fired with H.E. Shell at regular intervals during day & in the afternoon the Heavy Battery fired on enemy's parapet opposite 56.57.58 with great effect. The splinters in some cases coming back over our parapet (300 yds) At 7 pm 2 Coy T.M. Gun & Snipers left trenches & returned to billets. 2/Lt J.C. Cameron granted leave to U.K. 12th to 19th Sept. Fine – Warm Orders received re expected move of 27th Div. to new area. All leave being held over.	Our Artillery

2nd Battalion The Queen's Own Cameron Highlanders.

Hour, Date, and Place	Summary of Events and Information	Remarks and References to Appendices
TRENCHES (LA VESÉE) 13th Sept. Mon. 1915	Bn. occupied trenches. At 10 a.m H.Q & Coy Commanders 7th Yorkshire Regt (19th Bde 23rd Div) visited trenches. At 4.45 a.m a heavy detonation as of mine exploding was felt & immediately volumes of smoke & dust came down the line from the left. Enemy at once opened heavy bombardment on trenches Rue de Bois, gradually working along line to T.5? & Bn H.Q in rear. Fire was kept up for about 20 minutes. Our batteries was called on & after a short interval opened fire. Enemy's fire gradually slackened off & finally ceased about 5.20 a.m. At 11 a.m our Arty commenced firing & enemy immediately replied. The H.Q line parapet was damaged in places & one man killed. At 7 pm H.Q & 2 Coys 7th Yorks came in for instn. & were distributed 2 platoons per trench. Casualties Killed 17183 Pte R. Shearer D. Coy. (S)	

2nd Battalion The Queen's Own Cameron Highlanders.

Hour, Date, and Place	Summary of Events and Information	Remarks and References to Appendices
TRENCHES (LA VESÉE) 14th Sept. Tues 1915	Bn occupied trenches. Throughout the day our artillery continued to register on enemy's trenches. At 7.15 pm H.Q & 2 Coy E/Yorks were relieved by M.Gun & 2 Coys same regiment who were distributed as before to trenches. 2 Lt Napier returned from attachment to R.E. Fine — Cool.	

2nd Battalion The Queen's Own Cameron Highlanders.

Hour, Date, and Place	Summary of Events and Information	Remarks and References to Appendices
TRENCHES (LA VESÉE) To HUTS. (ERQUINGHEM.) 15th Sept. Wed. 1915	Bn. was relieved at 7 pm by 8th Yorks. The M.G. & two coys. already in trenches under instruction taking over T.56 & 55½ + support platoons, the other two coys T.58 & 57. Relief complete at 10.30 pm except Signallers who were relieved later. No casualties. Some shelling during day which accounted for an officer 7/Yorks badly hit by splinter in T.57 & one man Cameron slightly hit. On completion of relief Coys. marched independently to billets in huts at Erquinghem. Casualties Wounded 8647 Pte J. Watson D. Coy. (S) Duty Fine Cool	

2nd Battalion The Queen's Own Cameron Highlanders.

Hour, Date, and Place	Summary of Events and Information	Remarks and References to Appendices
HUTS (ERQUINGHEM) 18th October 1915	Bn. remained in huts. Orders received for move the following day. Fine cool	

2nd Battalion The Queen's Own Cameron Highlanders.

Hour, Date, and Place	Summary of Events and Information	Remarks and References to Appendices
HUTS (ERQUINGHEM) To BIVOUAC (VIEUX BERQUIN) 17th Sept 1915	Bn paraded at 5.20 am & marched to Bivouac & Billets South of VIEUX BERQUIN (10½ miles) where they arrived at 8.45. All Bns of Bde marched independently with their transport - Bde HQ. moved from STEENWERCK to VIEUX-BERQUIN. No men fell out. Fine - warm	

2nd Battalion The Queen's Own Cameron Highlanders.

Hour, Date, and Place	Summary of Events and Information	Remarks and References to Appendices
BIVOUAC (VIEUX BERQUIN) 18th Sept Sat 1915	Bn. remained in Bivouac. At 9.15 am Bn. marched to a point of assembly near VIEUX BERQUIN where Lt Gen Sir W Pulteney KCB DSO Commdg. III Corps made a farewell address, complimenting Bde on the work done since arrival at ARMENTIERES and telling us that the Div" was moving South to form part of a new corps which would take over some of the French line E of AMIENS. Orders received for entrainment on 19th @ HAZEBROUCK Stn. Fine - warm	

Attached Appx

2nd Battalion The Queen's Own Cameron Highlanders.

Hour, Date, and Place	Summary of Events and Information	Remarks and References to Appendices
VIEUX BERQUIN TO HAZEBROUCK 19th Sept. Sunday 1915	Bn remained in Bivouac until 4.30 pm when Coys paraded & Bn marched to HAZEBROUCK (5¼ m) & entrained at 7.45 pm. Composition of train 25 Trucks for men holding 35 each, 9 Trucks for animals holding 6 Heavy Draught or 8 light draught each, 12 vehicles for wagons & carts. Also an Officers Coach. Transport was sent to Stn with loading party 3 hours earlier. Two Platoons A Coy were left in Bivouac there being no accommodation for them in train. Train left @ 9.9 pm. Fine Cool	

A.B.Whey
Adjt

2nd Battalion The Queen's Own Cameron Highlanders.

Hour, Date, and Place	Summary of Events and Information	Remarks and References to Appendices
WARFUSÉE – ABANCOURT 20th Sept Mon 1915	At 9.30 am train arrived at GUILLANCOURT (3 hours late) where Bn detrained. After making teas & having breakfast Bn paraded & marched to ABANCOURT about 5 miles. The 1 R S having preceded Bn were already in the village the 1 Wiltsh Rs, 79 Worcesters & 9th R Scots followed the Bn in that order. Men were Bivouaced in field HQ & A Coys billetted in the village. Village situated about 15 miles due E of Amiens. And about 10 miles N from Trench line. Country round open rolling plains very little cover. Soil chalk. Water scarce except in River Canal 2½ miles N. At 7.30 pm Lt Tucker & 50 men B. Coy ordered to report @ XIII Corps HQ VILLERS BRETONNEUX 5 miles N. 27th Divn now serving in 13th Corps 3rd Army. Fine Cool	

A Macking
O.C.

2nd Battalion The Queen's Own Cameron Highlanders.

Hour, Date, and Place	Summary of Events and Information	Remarks and References to Appendices
ABANCOURT 21st Sept Tues 1915	Bn remained in house & Billets. Transport moved out 2½ m. N. to CERISE owing to scarcity of water in village. Fine Cool	

2nd Battalion The Queen's Own Cameron Highlanders.

Hour, Date, and Place	Summary of Events and Information	Remarks and References to Appendices
ABANCOURT 22nd Sept 1915	Bn. remained in Billets. 1/R.S. & bn MORCOURT 5 m. Battle now in	Original Bn letter notes N.E. Div. Reserve.
	Fine Cool	

2nd Battalion The Queen's Own Cameron Highlanders.

Gale & Polden, Ltd., Printers, Aldershot. 1043.-w.

Hour, Date, and Place	Summary of Events and Information	Remarks and References to Appendices
ABANCOURT 23rd Sept Thurs 1915	Bn remained in Bivouac until late in afternoon when the Coys moved into billets. These were found to be extraordinarily dirty & in most cases quite unfit for occupation until cleaned & disinfected. Accommodation very limited. At 4pm 2/Cameron & 1/Argyll & Sutherland High[rs] were inspected by Lt Gen Sir Charles C Munro K.C.B. G.O.C. 3rd Army, who expressed his approval at the appearance & general turn out of the two Battns. Fine in morning. Rain commenced at 7pm & continued all night. O.B.	

2nd Battalion The Queen's Own Cameron Highlanders.

Gale & Polden, Ltd., Printers, Aldershot. 1043.-w.

Hour, Date, and Place	Summary of Events and Information	Remarks and References to Appendices
ABANCOURT 24th Sept. 1915	Bn remained in billets. Wet & cold	

	Off	OR	Horses	M.G.	Web.	2Wh	b.		Attached Other Units	O	OR
Effective Strength	29	963		4	21	4	6		Gas Coy 3rd q		4
Attached	1	1						No rations	Cadet School		1
									3rd Corps H.Q.		4
War Estab.	30	1001		4	21	4	9		171 Coy RE		1
To Complete		37					3		187 — —		23
Surplus									M.M.P.		1
									Not included in ✱		34
Attached	1							Chaplain	27th Div Train		5
Sick & Base		72							XII Corps H.Q.	1	50
									Div. H.Q.		3
									" Sanitation		4
Strength	31	1036							Bde H.Q.		7
									Wessex RE		1
									G.H.Q.		1
									Included in ✱	1	71

AMcInnes
adjt

2nd Battalion The Queen's Own Cameron Highlanders.

Hour, Date, and Place	Summary of Events and Information	Remarks and References to Appendices
ABANCOURT To. PROYART 25th Sept. Sat. 1915	At 12.30 pm orders were received that Bn would vacate billets & move to TROYART - about 6 miles due East. Coys moved off independently owing the exposed nature of Country. D Coy at 2.30 pm A,B,C, grenadiers & M.G. in that order at ¼ hrs interval. Transport was ordered in from CERISY, picked up kits & followed the M Gun. Billeting party preceded Bn, but owing to complete lack of arrangements by Divn Staff it was some hours after arrival of last party that all were accommodated. Information received of successful advance made by 1st Army & French Troops both N. & South. Rain Cool. Lt Tucker & 5 men one of 50 return from XII Corps H.Q. 16 miners sent to CAPPY to form Div tunnelling Section.	

2nd Battalion The Queen's Own Cameron Highlanders.

Hour, Date, and Place	Summary of Events and Information	Remarks and References to Appendices
PROYART 26th Sept Sunday 1915	Bn remained in billets. In the afternoon 81 Bde HQ arrived from ABANCOURT & billeted in village. Fine Cool.	

2nd Battalion The Queen's Own Cameron Highlanders.

Hour, Date, and Place	Summary of Events and Information	Remarks and References to Appendices
PROYART 27th Sept. Mon. 1915	Bn. remained in billets. Information received of continued successes of French & British. Large numbers (21000) unwounded prisoners reported captured. Casualty 181 Coy R.E. tunnelling Coy. Wounded 16407 Pte J. Cooper A Coy. Wet Cold	

2nd Battalion The Queen's Own Cameron Highlanders.

Hour, Date, and Place	Summary of Events and Information	Remarks and References to Appendices
PROYART 25th Sept. Tues. 1915	Bn remained in billets. Continued successes of Allies reported on both fronts. Lt Col J D McLachlan heard unofficially that he had been appointed to 8th Bde - with rank of Brig¹ General.	

2nd Battalion The Queen's Own Cameron Highlanders.

Hour, Date, and Place	Summary of Events and Information	Remarks and References to Appendices
PROYART 29th Sept Wed 1915	Bn remained in billets. 2/Lt P Graham to Hospt (temperature)	
	Some rain. V. cold	
Hawking at 7h		

2nd Battalion The Queen's Own Cameron Highlanders.

Hour, Date, and Place	Summary of Events and Information	Remarks and References to Appendices
PROYART. 30th Sept Thurs. 1915	Bn. remained in billets. Dry. cold.	
	(signed) Adjt.	

81st Inf.Bde.
27th Div.

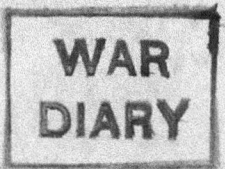

2nd BATTN. THE QUEEN'S OWN CAMERON HIGHLANDERS.

O C T O B E R

1 9 1 5

2nd Battalion The Queen's Own Cameron Highlanders.

Hour, Date, and Place	Summary of Events and Information	Remarks and References to Appendices
PROYART 1st Oct. Friday 1915	Bn. remained in billets. Lt. Col. J.E. McLachlan left to take over command of 8th Infy. Brigade. The following farewell order was published: "Lieut Colonel J.E. McLachlan on giving up command of the Battalion wishes to thank the Officers, Warrant Officers, Non Commissioned officers & men of the battn. for their loyal & unfailing support throughout the period during which it has been his privilege to command them. He is sure that his promotion to command a brigade is due to the valour and efficiency of the battalion and is a tribute to its work. He is proud of having commanded so fine a body of men; he parts from them with regret, and he wishes them one and all the very best of happiness and good fortune" 2/Lt. P. Graham returned to duty from Hosp¹. Fane - Col.	

2nd Battalion The Queen's Own Cameron Highlanders.

Gale & Polden, Ltd., Printers, Aldershot. 1043.-w.

Hour, Date, and Place	Summary of Events and Information	Remarks and References to Appendices
PROYART 2nd Oct. Sat 1915	Bn. remained in billets. Major and Adjutant A.D. Macpherson assumed command of the Battalion — Captain A.C. Lampson took over the duties of Senior Major, Lieut R.D. Wylie took over command and payment of D. Coy from Captain A.C. Lampson, & Lieut C.M. Mills took over the duties of A/Adjutant 2/Lieut J. Moffat was placed in temporary command of the Grenadier Company vice Lieut C.M. Mills. 2/Lieut P. Graham proceeded to H.Q. 3rd Wing R.F.C. to interview the Commandant with a view to his transfer to that branch of the service. 100 men on R.E. fatigue Dull - cold	

2nd Battalion The Queen's Own Cameron Highlanders.

HOUR, DATE, AND PLACE	SUMMARY OF EVENTS AND INFORMATION	REMARKS AND REFERENCES TO APPENDICES
PROYART 3rd Oct: Sunday 1915	Bn remained in billets. Rev. A.S.G. Gilchrist conducted Divine Service. Major General McCracken 27th Div attended the service and afterwards spoke to the officers of the Battalion. Fine - warmer 50 men on R.E. fatigue	

2nd Battalion The Queen's Own Cameron Highlanders.

Hour, Date, and Place	Summary of Events and Information	Remarks and References to Appendices
PROYART 6th Oct. Mon 1915	Bn remained in billets. One Coy billeted at PROYART the remainder of Battn. at MORCOURT. The 81st Bde. took over right section of trenches from 82nd Bde occupying trenches H.2 - H.1 - G.2 - G.2 - G.1 - 7.2 in front of DOMPIERRE. 1st Royal Scots & 2nd Glo'sters went in. The 9th R. Scots moving 2 Coys to FONTAINE-LES-CAPPY and 2 Coys to CHUIGNES. The 1st Argyll & Sutherland Hghrs. moved from ABANCOURT to CHUIGNOLLES and the Bde H.Q. moved from PROYART to CHUIGNOLLES. The Battn. remained in PROYART. 10 Signallers arrived from Invergordon. About 200 men on RE fatigue. Some rain - Cold	

2nd Battalion The Queen's Own Cameron Highlanders.

Hour, Date, and Place	Summary of Events and Information	Remarks and References to Appendices
PROYART 5th Oct. Tues. 1915	Bn remained in billets. 50 men on R.E. fatigue. O.C. 91st Bgd. in command visited trenches. Very wet & cold	

2nd Battalion The Queen's Own Cameron Highlanders.

Hour, Date, and Place	Summary of Events and Information	Remarks and References to Appendices
PROYART 1st Oct Wed 1915	Bn. remained in billets. Coy. Commanders visited trenches. Working party 200 men B & C Coy. under R.E. during the night in Glo'ster trenches. Fine + Cold	

2nd Battalion The Queen's Own Cameron Highlanders.

Hour, Date, and Place	Summary of Events and Information	Remarks and References to Appendices
PROYART 7th Oct: Thurs 1915	Bn remained in billets. Draft of 16 rejoined from base. Transport moved to CHIGNOLLES.	

2nd Battalion The Queen's Own Cameron Highlanders.

Gale & Polden, Ltd., Printers, Aldershot. 1043.-w.

Hour, Date, and Place	Summary of Events and Information	Remarks and References to Appendices
PROYART. To TRENCHES (Dompierre Sect) 8th Oct: 1915	Bn marched by coys at 5 minutes interval via CHUIGNOLLES to head of C.C. trench. Relief of 7/R. Scots commenced at 10 a.m. & was completed about 12 noon. No casualties. Coys occupied trenches H2 - H1 - G3 which were held by A. B. D. coys respectively, C Coy in support between Bn Hq & trenches. C. Coy & Bn Hq. 5th R Scots Fusiliers came in with relief for instruction, being distributed a platoon to each Coy. Trenches in fair condition except front-line which was much knocked about & could only be held very lightly, principally by listening posts. French miners still at work on mines. Evidence of result of mining operation by enemy in the past very apparent - ground between trenches, which were only 40 yds apart in places, pitted with craters. Casualties Wounded 17272 Pte G. Buchanan B Coy Duty 8566 L/C W Drendon A " (Self) Fine cold	

2nd Battalion The Queen's Own Cameron Highlanders.

Hour, Date, and Place	Summary of Events and Information	Remarks and References to Appendices
TRENCHES (Sompierre) 9th Dec. Sat. 1915	Bn occupied Trenches. Enemy quiet except for some bombing & trench mortar fire to which we replied. A feature of the trench line was the size & depth of the dug-outs constructed by the French - which were made to a depth of 15 feet below ground. As a general rule the roofs were domed which apparently in the loam soil does away with necessity of supports & revetting. Casualties Wounded 7324 Sgt J Cameron B. Coy. 5847 A/C R Boyd B. "	

Fine Cold

	Off.	O.R.	Horses	Rg	4Wh 2Wh	6		Attached O.R. not (Cams)	O.R.
Effective Strength	29	969	73	4	19	4	9	Gen Coy	4
War Estab	30	1001	78	4	21	4	9	Cadet Scheme	1
To Complete	1	32	5		2			171 Coy RE	23
								101 —	1
								114 D	
Non-Combatant		52						Bde Mining	16
								12 Coyt	4
Attached	1						Chapn	T Bde	2
									32
Base & Hospt		56						27 Div Train	6
								Div HQ	3
Strength	29	1077						Bde Batn	4
								Sur. Sect	4
								2nd RE	1
								RMP	1
								Bomb School	11
								Salvage Coy	2
									57

A D McKay
Command.

2nd Battalion The Queen's Own Cameron Highlanders.

Hour, Date, and Place	Summary of Events and Information	Remarks and References to Appendices
TRENCHES (Dompierre) 10th Oct. Sunday 1915	Bn. occupied trenches. Some light shelling & trench mortar fire exchanged. "C" Coy & H.q. 5th R.S.F. returned to billets. Fine - warmer	

2nd Battalion The Queen's Own Cameron Highlanders.

Hour, Date, and Place	Summary of Events and Information	Remarks and References to Appendices
TRENCHES (Vermelles) 11th Oct 1915	Bn occupied trenches. Line extended by 150 yds to left for which purpose one platoon of "C" Coy in support were moved forward. A quiet day - some very heavy Trench Mortar bombs put into B Coy's trench, 2 of which exploded but without doing any damage. Some rain. Warmer.	

2nd Battalion The Queen's Own Cameron Highlanders.

Hour, Date, and Place	Summary of Events and Information	Remarks and References to Appendices
TRENCHES (Tompraison) TO PROYART. 12th Oct. Tues 1915	Bn. was relieved by 1/R Scots at 10 am. Relief completed by 12 noon. Coys marched independently to billets the last Coy getting in about 2.30 pm. Casualty. Wounded 17830 Pte A. Mitchell C. Coy S.I. Orders received that from 13th the Bn. would be attached to 67th Bde. 22nd Divn. replacing 7th S.W. Borderers who would be temporarily attached to 81st Bde. The same arrangements being made with 7th Bde. 67th Bde comprising 4th K.R.R.C, 2/Cameron H'rs, Cambridgeshire Regt (T.), 7th S.W. Borderers (K), & 11th R. Welsh Fusiliers (K). Attachments to be for 14 days. True Warner	

2nd Battalion The Queen's Own Cameron Highlanders.

Hour, Date, and Place	Summary of Events and Information	Remarks and References to Appendices
PROYART 13th Oct. 1915	Bn. remained in billets. Transport moved from CHUIGNOLLES to PROYART. Baths were arranged for ½ Bn. at PROYART & MORCOURT. D. Coy employed on digging defensive line N.E. of PROYART. Bn. attached to 67th Bde 22nd Div.	

2nd Battalion The Queen's Own Cameron Highlanders.

Hour, Date, and Place	Summary of Events and Information	Remarks and References to Appendices
PROYART 14th Oct. Thurs 1915	Bn. remained in billets. Conference of COs with Brig'r at MORCOURT. In the afternoon C.O. & some officers Welsh Fus. came over from ABANCOURT to discuss system of work carried out by Batt'n. Remainder of Batt'n worked at obtaining change of clothing. Digging continued, each Coy employing 2 platoons in relief of 4 hrs during day on defensive line.	

2nd Battalion The Queen's Own Cameron Highlanders.

Hour, Date, and Place	Summary of Events and Information	Remarks and References to Appendices
PROYART 15th Oct Frid 1915	Bn. remained in billets. Work on defensive line NE of PROYART continued as before. Orders received that 67th Bde would take over FRISE section of Trenches from 80th Bde on 16th. 4th KRRC, Cambridgeshire Regt & 7th S.W.B. to take over trenches & 2/Cameron & 11th R.W.Fus. to take over billets in CAPPY. All Transport to move to BRAY. Fine cool	

	Off	OR	Ammn	Reg	4xxx	2xxx	6		Attach'd 6 O.V.Rutl.(Cdn) O. OR	
Effective Strength	29	957	72	4	19	4	9		Gds Coy	4
War Estab.	30	1001	78	4	21	4	9		171 Coy RE	1
To complete	1	44	6	✓	✓	✓	✓		152 " "	23
									MMP	1
On Command		51							Bde Miners	16
Attached	1							Chaplain	Sig. Corps	3
									P. Bde	2
									Base Details	1
Sick & Base		64								51
Strength	29	1072							27 Dn Train	5
									Div. Hq	4
									" Ordnance	1
									Bde Hq	6
									Divers RE	1
									PMP	1
									Leave	8
									Bomb School	11
									Proyart Bakery	4
									Sanit. Sect	4
									Salvage Coy	2
										51

2nd Battalion The Queen's Own Cameron Highlanders.

Hour, Date, and Place	Summary of Events and Information	Remarks and References to Appendices
PROYART To CAPPY 16th Oct. Sat 1915	At 1.35 pm Bn. marched to CAPPY arriving there at 3 pm where billets were taken over from 7/K.S.L.I. Billets on the whole clean with some notable exceptions chiefly Coy. H.Qrs. 67th Inf Bde took over trenches as shown in orders of 15th. Two M.guns with teams were ordered to relieve M.guns of 8/KRRC (70th Bde) in support line. Fine. Cool	

2nd Battalion The Queen's Own Cameron Highlanders.

Hour, Date, and Place	Summary of Events and Information	Remarks and References to Appendices
CAPPY. 17th Oct Sunday 1915	Bn remained in billets. Divine Service held @ 10 am. In the afternoon an exchange was made with 11th R.W.F. of 4 Platoon Officers - 2 C.S.M - 2 C.Sgts. - 4 Sergeants with the object of instructing her Bn in system of work in & out of the trenches.	Fine - Cold

2nd Battalion The Queen's Own Cameron Highlanders.

Hour, Date, and Place	Summary of Events and Information	Remarks and References to Appendices
CAPPY 18th Oct. Mon. 1915	Bn. remained in billets. 60 men of Bn. bathed at CAPPY. 200 men were employed on work in front trenches FRISE Sector in two reliefs by day - one casualty. And 50 men in right Sector by night. Casualty. Killed 5175 Pte A. McLean A Coy (Shell) Fine - Cold	2/Lt Collinson proceeded on leave UK 18th - 25th

A.D.W.May
Commdg

2nd Battalion The Queen's Own Cameron Highlanders.

Hour, Date, and Place	Summary of Events and Information	Remarks and References to Appendices
CAPPY 19th Oct. Tues 1915	Bn. remained in billets. 200 men employed on work in front line of Right Sector by day. C.O. & Coy Commdrs. visited R. Sector trenches with a view to taking over on night 20/21	Fine - Cold

2nd Battalion The Queen's Own Cameron Highlanders.

HOUR, DATE, AND PLACE	SUMMARY OF EVENTS AND INFORMATION	REMARKS AND REFERENCES TO APPENDICES
CAPPY 20th Oct. Wed 1915	Bn. remained in billets. Rev. A.J. Gilchrist proceeded on leave to U.K. 20th - 27th Oct. At 1.45 pm orders re relief of 7 SWB in trenches cancelled & Bn ordered to stand-by ready to move to Huts FROISSY. No move however took place that day. Fine cold Bn rejoined 81st from attachment to 67th Inf Bde. which returned to 22nd Divn. 4 officers, 2 C Sms, 2 C Qms, 4 NCOs rejoined from attachment between 9 Camerons & 11 R.W. Fus. All leave cancelled (this not affecting Padre Gilchrist)	

2nd Battalion The Queen's Own Cameron Highlanders.

Hour, Date, and Place	Summary of Events and Information	Remarks and References to Appendices
CAPPY 21st Oct. Thurs 1915	Bn. remained in billets. Move to FROISSY cancelled. Operation order reference relief of British line by French Troops received & probable date of move & direction thereof notified. Fine - heavy rain at night - cold.	

2nd Battalion The Queen's Own Cameron Highlanders.

HOUR, DATE, AND PLACE	SUMMARY OF EVENTS AND INFORMATION	REMARKS AND REFERENCES TO APPENDICES
CAPPY 12th October 1915	Bn. remained in billets. Leave reopened to 40 Men. On working parties assisting miners in Dompierre Section. Fine - Cold	billets. 27th Divl working party assisting Section.

	Off	OR	Animals	MG	4wh	2wh	B		Attach'd Other Units (Armies)	O	OR
Effective Strength	29	952	74	4	19	4	9		Gas Coy		4
War Estab	30	1001	78	4	21	4	9		171 Coy RE		1
To Complete	1	49	4		2				173 - -		23
Command		51							MGB		
Attached	1							Chaplain	Bde Miners		18
									X Corps		3
									9 Bde		2
									Base Prison		1
Sick + Base		59									57
Strength	29	1062							27 Div Train		5
									HQ		3
									Ordnance		4
									9 Bde HQ		7
									Wessex RE		7
									MP		1
									Leave	1	13
										1	34

2nd Battalion The Queen's Own Cameron Highlanders.

Hour, Date, and Place	Summary of Events and Information	Remarks and References to Appendices
CAPPY 23rd Oct: Sat 1915	Bn. remained in billets. All men on extra regimental employment within Divn. area, except B.de & Divn HQ staff employ., returned to Battn. Operation orders for move to WARFUSÉE-ABANCOURT on Sunday, 24th received. Fine - Cold	

2nd Battalion The Queen's Own Cameron Highlanders.

Hour, Date, and Place	Summary of Events and Information	Remarks and References to Appendices
CAPPY to WARFUSÉE-ABANCOURT 24th Oct: Sunday 1915	At 12 noon Bn marched to ABANCOURT arriving there at 3.45 pm (10½ m) and occupying old billets in that place. 1st line Transport marched with Bn. Two Baggage wagons moved independently & blankets were sent forward on a motor lorry. This was necessitated by withdrawal of the two blanket wagons in the Spring, which had never been replaced. 4 men fell out from Coys & marched with Transport. Capt R Letton proceeded on leave to UK. 24th – 31st Oct. Ramey – Col¹ The Brigade was relieved by the French. Bde HQ remaining at CHUIGNOLLES, Cameron & Argyll Sutherland Hghrs & 9/R Scots marched to ABANCOURT – 1/R Scots & 9/10 Stirrs on being relieved in trenches marched to MORCOURT. During the period Divⁿ was in occupation of Trenches in this area. Bn only completed one tour (4 days) in actual occupation of the line.	

2nd Battalion The Queen's Own Cameron Highlanders.

Hour, Date, and Place	Summary of Events and Information	Remarks and References to Appendices
ABANCOURT 25th Oct. Mon. 1915	Bn. remained in billets. Operation orders for move to BOVES on Tues 26th received. Damp - Cold.	

2nd Battalion The Queen's Own Cameron Highlanders.

Hour, Date, and Place	Summary of Events and Information	Remarks and References to Appendices
ABANCOURT To BOVES 26th Oct: Tues. 1915	At 7.10 am Bn. marched to BOVES (9½ m) arriving there at 10.30 am. The remainder of Bde followed at short intervals. One man of Battn fell out on the march. Bde accommodated in camp. 2/Lt Collinson returned from leave. Fine v. Cold, Wet later. Blankets were carried on motor lorries.	

2nd Battalion The Queen's Own Cameron Highlanders.

Hour, Date, and Place	Summary of Events and Information	Remarks and References to Appendices
BOVES TO BOUGANVILLE 27th Oct: Wed 1915	At 7 am the Bde marched to billets 9/R Scots, Camerons, 1/A&SH to BOUGANVILLE, 4/R Scots to SAISSIVAL, Bde HQ & 2/9 10's etc to SEUX. An interval of 15 minutes was allowed between Bns, but in the case of the first 3 mentioned this was decreased owing to delays on the part of 9/R.S. transport. The road was of good surface but very hilly. Distance to BOUGANVILLE 17 miles. One man in Bn. fell out. Comparative table of men falling out on 26 & 27th shown as follows: 26th 27th 4/R.S. 9 25 = 34 9/R.S. 7 12 = 19 2/9.R. 4 9 = 13 2/C.H. 1 1 = 2 1/A&SH 3 10 = 13 Bn arrived in billets at 2:45pm, the march having been continued without a halt for dinners as was done by other Bns. Wet, cold. Blankets were carried on motor lorries.	

2nd Battalion The Queen's Own Cameron Highlanders.

Hour, Date, and Place	Summary of Events and Information	Remarks and References to Appendices
BOUGANVILLE TO ST AUBIN 28th Oct. Thurs. 1915	At 2 pm. Bn. moved to St AUBIN (3½m) arriving at 3 pm. Rev. Gilchrist returned from leave. Wet. Cold.	new billets in at 3 pm. from leave.

2nd Battalion The Queen's Own Cameron Highlanders.

Hour, Date, and Place	Summary of Events and Information	Remarks and References to Appendices
St AUBIN 29th Oct. Tue. 1917	Bn. remained in billets Lt. T.O. Macleod proceeded on leave to U.K. 30th to 7th Nov. Fine - Cold	

	Off	OR	animals	rg	4 wh	2wh	b			
Effective Strength	29	956	74	4	19	4	9	Attach'd O units (train)	O	OR
War Estab	30	1001	78	4	21	4	9	Gas Coy		4
To Complete	1	45	4	✓	2	✓	✓	17 Coy RE		1
Command		37						TT		23
Attached	1							MFP		1
Sick T/Base		68						XII Corps		2
Strength	29	1061						17 Bde		2
								Base Prison		2
								27 Div Base (for discharge)		1
					Chaplain			M.T. ASC		1
										37
								27 Div Train		5
								— HQ		3
								Ordnance		4
								Bde HQ		6
								Wewer RE		1
								GMP		1
								Leave	2	11
									2	31

2nd Battalion The Queen's Own Cameron Highlanders.

Hour, Date, and Place	Summary of Events and Information	Remarks and References to Appendices
St AUBIN 30th Oct. Sat 1915	Bn. remained in billets.	Fine — a little warmer (rain at night.)

2nd Battalion The Queen's Own Cameron Highlanders.

Hour, Date, and Place	Summary of Events and Information	Remarks and References to Appendices
St AUBIN 31st Oct - Sunday 1915	Bn remained in billets 2/Lt MacLeod proceeded to UK 31st – 7th Nov. Rain - cold.	on leave

H. Dm. Maj
Comndg

WAR DIARY

www.ingramcontent.com/pod-product-compliance
Lightning Source LLC
Chambersburg PA
CBHW080829010526
44112CB00015B/2479